P9-AGH-225

the

POWER

of

KNITTING

Stitching Together
Our Lives *in a* Fractured World

Loretta Napoleoni

A TARCHERPERIGEE BOOK

an imprint of Penguin Random House LLC

penguinrandomhouse.com

Published in Swedish as *Att sticka för livet* by Mondial and in Italian as *Sul filo di lana* by Mondadori, in 2019.

Copyright © 2020 by Loretta Napoleoni

All the patterns in this book have been tested, knitted, and in some cases adapted by Il Caffè dei Gomitoli of Cristina Longati in Bologna, in collaboration with Maglialenta of Grazia Baravelli

Illustrations by Alessandra Olanow / Illustration Division, Inc.

www.ilcaffedeigomitoli.it

TarcherPerigee with tp colophon is a registered trademark of Penguin Random House LLC

Most TarcherPerigee books are available at special quantity discounts for bulk purchase for sales promotions, premiums, fund-raising, and educational needs. Special books or book excerpts also can be created to fit specific needs. For details, write: SpecialMarkets@penguinrandomhouse.com.

Library of Congress Cataloging-in-Publication Data
Names: Napoleoni, Loretta, author.
Title: The power of knitting : stitching together our lives in a fractured world / by Loretta Napoleoni.
Description: [New York] : TarcherPerigee, an imprint of Penguin Random House LLC, [2020] | Includes bibliographical references.
Identifiers: LCCN 2020000683 (print) | LCCN 2020000684 (ebook) | ISBN 9780593087190 (hardcover) | ISBN 9780593087206 (ebook)
Subjects: LCSH: Knitting. | Knitting—Patterns.
Classification: LCC TT820 .N364 2020 (print) | LCC TT820 (ebook) | DDC 746.43/2—dc23
LC record available at https://lccn.loc.gov/2020000683
LC ebook record available at https://lccn.loc.gov/2020000684
p.   cm.

Printed in China

1 3 5 7 9 10 8 6 4 2

Book design by Lorie Pagnozzi

33614082108282

TO MY SON JULIAN, THE NEEDLE
I USED TO STITCH MY LIFE
BACK TOGETHER

CONTENTS

When personal catastrophe struck, I turned to the disciplines of my profession—economics, politics, the social sciences—to help me piece my life back together. I soon realized that these fields of knowledge and wisdom were not enough for such a challenging task. I needed something stronger, something universal, something that would keep me anchored to the beauty of life, a powerful, positive instrument to give me courage and hope. As I looked back at my life, at the many lessons I received when I was a child to prepare me to navigate it, I realized that knitting had been my constant companion, a craft I shared with those I love and who love me, a tangible activity that has kept me connected to the universal, positive attributes of humanity.

In the virtual world, images, texts, and voices reach us in real time through the screens of our smartphones, tablets, and computers. Yet these are little more than mere exchanges among machines and microchips. In the sterile, cold, cyber universe we inhabit, people touch, smell, kiss, and hug each other less and less; our connections are sense-deprived.

We are physically detached. I am physically detached. I can Skype with my children across the world every day, but I do not hug them for months on end. And I miss them deeply.

In the early 1990s, a major political event reshaped my life. The Red Brigades, the Italian Marxist group, declared an end to their armed struggle and began talking to a few select people about their experience. I was one of those people. To conduct my investigation, I left my job as an economist with the City of London and spent years interviewing members of armed organizations. When I realized it is economics more than politics that influences their behavior, I focused my work on their financing. Then 9/11 happened, and my research, knowledge, and insight into the funding of armed groups became very valuable to those who wanted to understand and fight modern terrorism.

As the war on terror took shape, coupled with the advent of "virtual life" and globalization, the world was forced into a major transformation. Fear and isolation became the demons of the new millennium. I wrote several books to bear witness to these extraordinary and painful changes of the last twenty years. Rereading some of them made me realize that society is not coping with the current transition we are undergoing. To rebalance our personal and public lives, we must heal the hurts we have suffered and shield ourselves from future damage. The challenge we face is so unconventional that psychology, politics, and economics, the traditional tools used to cure societies' malaise, are useless. Because we are sailing in uncharted waters, we must find alternative skills with which to navigate our present journey; we need to experiment with unexpected forms of healing. In other words, we must think outside the box.

Even in our private lives, physical isolation and virtual communication impair traditional social behavior. Because we do not know how to behave during this transformational time, society has become increasingly dysfunctional and people have become delusional. I realized this for myself when my husband brought me and our family to the brink of financial ruin at the end of the 2010s and I had to reinvent my life one more time.

I feel like an old but strong yarn in the hands of a mediocre and insecure knitter who keeps making big mistakes and changing her mind about what to knit. I have been knitted, undone, and reknitted several times over. I have been washed, stretched, and dried before being restitched and re-purled so often I have lost count. Each time, the pattern of life I must follow becomes more challenging, more demanding, and yet I have managed to perform almost as well as a brand-new yarn. But this time is different, this is the last attempt, I have reached my limit, I must get the pattern right.

The world we inhabit, including my own personal and professional worlds, is voyeuristic, antisocial, and highly technological. It is lonely and full of existential cracks, fractured, and it takes less than a second to fall into one of its crevasses. Could this be the root cause of the existential malaise that plagues us all?

I long for the warm coziness of intimacy and safety, the sole antidotes for the chronic cybersolitude we suffer from. It was knitting that gave me a way out of the abyss, helping me to climb back up. Teaching a close friend's child how to knit one day brought back the memory of when my own grandmother first put a knitting needle in my hands. The wool, the pattern, the excitement of the long and skinny metal rod in my goddaughter's little hands, my fingers over hers: Everything was the same. I was performing an ancient ritual of initiation, a ceremony immune to time and technology. *I am not alone, I am the stitch between two beautiful purls, between my grandmother and my goddaughter, and together we are a knit stitch in the great pattern of social history.*

Alessandra Olanow, the illustrator of this book, shares my views. She accepted the invitation to participate in this project because knitting had created a special bond for her between her dying mother and the daughter in Alessandra's own womb. For months, she had knit for her baby at her mother's bedside, and the yarn became the link, the connection between the two women she most loves.

I reknit my life from ground zero while researching and writing this book. But this is neither a book about me nor just a book of knitting patterns. Each chapter will have just one pattern, which symbolizes its message; all the other images refer to knitted items I cared about and have lost during my lifetime.

This is the story of a remarkable craft, a much-needed social healer that reminds us that to exist, we need each other. Knitting is a good metaphor for our life; it can be related to everything we care about, from politics to economics to personal relationships. My aim is to address complex and often painful issues, both public and private, using knitting as a means to unravel and understand them. All we need to do to break free of our existential malaise is to keep purling and stitching, knitting our lives together.

the

POWER

of

KNITTING

Knitting
the Patterns *of*
Love, Politics,
and Economics

A headband, a light blue headband, was the first thing I knitted. I must have been six or seven years old when I picked up my first needles, under the supervision of my grandmother. If I close my eyes, I can still see, in the golden patina of my most precious memories, the two of us. We are sitting so close; her elbow is underneath mine, her large body warming my left side. I am excited. Somehow, I understand that this is a rite of passage, a tiny little step on my journey to becoming an adult, a woman, and I am eager to perform it. I am also nervous. I am pressing the yarn between my fingers with all my strength, as if in fear it will escape. My grandmother looks at me, smiles, and removes the yarn from my hand. Then she gently tucks one needle under my right arm, wraps my left hand around the other one, puts the yarn back in my right hand, and begins guiding me. *Relax*, she whispers, *do not pull the yarn too much or too little, let it be your friend, let it dance around the needles.*

And so my love story with knitting began.

I learned the times tables, memorized poems, and recited the rosary while knitting with my grandmother. Purls and stitches became numbers, words of beautiful sentences, Holy Marys and Our Fathers, all intertwined inside the magic fabric of our love. They connected her life to mine so that she could transmit her wisdom, so that her teachings could carry on guiding me forever in between stitches. Later on, in my twenties, as a passionate member of the feminist movement, I shared that insight with the traumatized women who sought help from our organization. Holding my needles and yarn, knitting the clothes I wore, I welcomed them to our consciousness-raising meetings.

My grandmother was born in 1900. She was fourteen when World War I broke out, eighteen when she met my grandfather, thirty-nine when World War II started, fifty-five when I was born, and fifty-nine when her husband died. She had witnessed the devastation of war not once but twice, endured Fascism, joined the Italian resistance, and seen the birth of the Italian democracy. She was a living history book I never grew tired of reading.

Her stories were amazing—scary, sad, and happy at the same time—but above all, they were real. She shared them with me while we knitted together. I was fascinated to hear about how the world had plunged into a global conflict and how her brothers and future husband had marched to the front to fight an evil enemy. There was such pride in her voice, a pride that blurred the horrors of the trenches, the cold, the mud, the hunger, the rats. She never tried to hide from me the terror of war, the inhumanity of the war front, but she put them in the context of the unpredictable patterns of life and politics. War was like a very, very difficult sequence of stitches. You could not skip one move; you had to tackle each one with courage and determination. I am thankful for her realism because it made me understand that peace is not a given and that if you want to protect it, you have to be an active member of society.

So in between purling and stitching, I fell in love with politics.

Naturally, in her stories my grandfather was the biggest hero. He fought in the Alps, in the Carso near the Austrian border, one of the toughest fronts of World War I. There, in the trenches, he met one of my grandmother's brothers, and they became good friends, so close that they shared the garments she had knit for her brother to wear at the front: the vests, socks, caps, scarves, and even long johns and sweaters that they wore under their uniforms in the freezing winter in the Dolomites.

In 1917, during an enemy attack, my grandmother's brother

was killed and my grandfather was seriously injured. When he finally recovered, the war was over. He decided to go to Rome to visit the family of his dead friend and to thank the mysterious woman who had kept him warm in the trenches. He brought her back the pair of thick, colorful striped socks he was wearing when a German grenade hit him, the only item remaining of those she had sent. He apologized to her for the bloodstains on them, which would not come out in the wash. She knew who he was from her brother's letters, but what she did not know is that while she had fallen in love with him while knitting warm garments, he had fallen in love with her while wearing them.

Knitting is an act of love, my grandmother used to say, perhaps to downplay in my eyes the uniqueness of her love story. She did not like to feel exceptional, to stand out. She was a

woman born at the beginning of the twentieth century; she had a specific place in society that demanded modesty, one she accepted without question. But with me, she could escape the female cage of her social status and open up her brilliant mind. On the wings of our needles, we flew high above the world to a special place that nobody knew.

I imagined it as a cozy knitted igloo in the middle of the North Pole.

There, in the emptiness of a sea of ice, we were free and warm and we could reinvent the world.

"Have I told you the true version of *Sleeping Beauty*?" she asked me one day as we were knitting a baby blanket for my cousin together. I looked at her with wide eyes, full of excitement, and shook my head. "If you remember," she began, "when Aurora was born, seven fairies were chosen to be her godmothers, but the king and queen forgot one, the oldest, because they thought she was dead.

"At Aurora's christening, to everyone's horror, the old fairy suddenly appeared. She was very, very angry. Instead of bringing a gift, she cursed the baby: at the age of sixteen, she foretold, Aurora would prick her finger on the spindle of a spinning wheel and die. Fortunately, the seventh fairy had still to offer her gift. She could not reverse the evil spell. However, she could mitigate it: Aurora would not die, but fall asleep for one hundred years until awakened by the kiss of a prince."

We both stopped knitting. I was so excited about what was coming next and my grandmother was so engaged in the rewriting of one of the most popular fairy tales that we had to rest our hands from directing the dance of the yarn around the needles.

"So?" I said.

"So," she continued, resuming her knitting, "to try to save his daughter from the terrible curse, the king ordered the people to destroy every spindle and spinning wheel in the kingdom in a gigantic bonfire. This was a huge mistake. The kingdom where Aurora was born was well known everywhere for its fine wool, silk, and beautiful knitted garments. People came from everywhere to purchase them and to trade with the kingdom. This was such a good and profitable business that most of the population earned their living in the wool and silk industries. The prohibition on spinning destroyed both, with terrible consequences for the kingdom's economy: Shepherds could not sell their wool and had to stop keeping their herds; silkworms were left unattended and died; knitters did not have access to yarns and stopped knitting. People grew cold and poor. As the years passed, a sense of bitterness plagued the kingdom; people began to resent the king for banning spinning. They lost trust in the community and took to stealing from each other what little they had left. The kingdom that at Aurora's birth was happy, rich, and friendly was, at her sixteenth birthday, a resentful, miserable, and freezing-cold place.

"Kept locked inside the castle to protect her from her destiny, Aurora did not know what was happening in the kingdom. She also had no idea she was the cause of such a transformation, as the king and the queen had prohibited everyone from telling her about the curse. The day of her sixteenth birthday, when she came upon an old lady in a little-used room in the castle, spinning wool and transforming it into yarn, she was immediately fascinated by such a metamorphosis and asked to try it herself.

"As she accidentally pricked her finger and the first drop of her blood spilled, staining the yarn, Aurora fell asleep. Distraught, the king and the queen placed their daughter on her bed in her chamber, covered her with their most precious knitted blanket, put a pink hat on her head to keep her warm, kissed her goodbye, and left the kingdom with heavy hearts. By the time Aurora woke up, they would be dead, and what would happen to their daughter then? The fairy godmother who had mitigated the curse had an idea: the kingdom had become a cold, broken-down village populated by desperate, unfriendly people; the countryside was bare because farmers had stopped farming; the woods were thick because nobody had been cutting trees; and soon whatever good was left in people would disappear. She could not leave Aurora in such a place for a hundred years. And so the fairy godmother cast a new spell. She put everyone to sleep, froze the kingdom, and made the forest trees grow so high that they hid the castle, leaving Aurora and the people to their long sleep.

"A hundred years passed without anyone approaching the kingdom, until a young prince, fascinated by the legends about a vanished kingdom that had produced the finest wool and silk garments in the world, decided to search for it. He traveled for years, all over the continent, until he met a very, very old man who guided him to the kingdom. That old man told him the legend of the sleeping princess.

"When the prince finally reached the castle, he looked for the room where Aurora was sleeping. As soon as he saw her, he fell in love. Overcome, he kissed her and broke the curse. Aurora and the prince soon married, and together they revived the wool and silk business of the kingdom, making it once more the finest producer in the world. The pink hat, in particular, was such a big hit that they decided to use it as the logo of their products. People prospered and were happy again," concluded my smiling grandmother.

And this is how I fell in love with economics while knitting.

Purl and stitch, stitch and purl, was also my laboratory for life. Each time I made a mistake, my grandmother told me to evaluate it: Can it be fixed without undoing some of the knitting,

or does it require drastic action? Mistakes must be addressed and solved, she repeated, because they will grow bigger and bigger as the knitting progresses. They will not disappear; on the contrary, they will stand out against the perfection of the rest of the work, and to fix them, you will need to undo so much more.

I wish I had followed her teaching when I saw the first signs of my husband's erratic behavior, small omens of his personal problems. A hole had appeared in the pattern of my marriage. I could not close it by picking up the missing stitches; to fix it, I had to undo my knitting. I knew this, but I chose to ignore it and kept purling and stitching in the hope that it would vanish— until the hole became so visible, so upsetting, that it overshadowed the beauty of my work.

A good knitter always has the courage to undo her work to fix a big mistake. A good knitter knows that everything can be mended as long as there is yarn and needles in her hands and courage in her heart to go back and start all over. A good knitter has wisdom.

I am not a good knitter. I am an okay knitter striving to get better and failing to do so rather often. But I am not a quitter. Having finally unraveled my marriage, I know that if I keep purling and stitching, remembering the teaching of my grandmother and of all the women before her who passed on their wisdom through the knitting needles, the pattern of my life will eventually improve.

I also know that I am not alone, not even in my personal difficulties. A magic yarn links all of us through time and space—all we need to do is pick it up and start knitting.

Why Do
We Knit?

The genesis of knitting is as unclear as the birth of the universe and the origins of the human race. We have no proof of when and how we began knitting; all we know for sure is that once it happened, it eventually became an integral part of human life. Just like the history of humanity, the history of knitting starts from chapter two, so chapter one is open to interpretations. This uncertainty can be comforting, as it allows most of us to write, or rewrite, the beginning of the story.

My grandmother, for example, believed in the "story of creation." God was so busy organizing everything for six whole days that on the seventh day, he had to rest, she used to say. But she could not resist altering some details of Genesis: Eve, who my grandmother never questioned had emerged from a rib of Adam, was too curious to keep from touching the apple tree. Eve took the apple because she wanted to taste it, not because someone convinced her to do so. The story of the snake, she told me, is a trick to make women look weak. (Naturally, she revealed this secret after my First Communion, to avoid confusing me during the lengthy preparation for it.) In other words, Eve was strong enough to exercise her free will. Adam, on the other hand, had none. As I grew older, her interpretation of Eve's disobedience offered me comfort and strength in a world still ruled by men; it made me believe in myself, follow my instincts, and conquer fear.

When investigating the genesis of knitting, one needs even more imagination. There is no mention of the craft in ancient books and chronicles, and the verb "to knit" is absent from pre-modern languages. We have to wait until the fifteenth century to find it in the *Oxford Unabridged English Dictionary* and until the Renaissance for it to become part of European languages. *Spinning* and *weaving* emerge much earlier, for they are regarded as noble crafts and have been celebrated in ancient poetry and literature.

Why is that?

Several decades ago, while traveling by bus in the Peruvian Andes, a French archaeology student offered what I still consider the best explanation: knitting is the proletariat craft.

His name was Philippe, and he was en route to Cuzco to meet a professor of archaeology with whom he had been in touch while researching his thesis on pre-Columbian crafts. I must confess that when he boarded the bus and sat next to me, the only Caucasian woman on board, I thought he looked like the typical French nerd: small glasses, brown suede shoes with laces, clean jeans, a white shirt, a dark green V-neck sweater, and a tight brown jacket. So I did not pay much attention when he introduced himself and began talking about the topic of his dissertation. It was only when he mentioned knitting that I joined him in what soon became a fascinating conversation.

According to Philippe, before spinning and weaving, people made fishing nets using a rudimentary form of knitting known as *nalbinding*, which he claimed was originally a Danish word. They used a single needle to hook together short lengths of very rough, unspun yarn. "You have seen it," he explained when I looked a bit puzzled, "it is what fisherman still use to repair fishing nets." The same technique was applied to produce cloth. "Think about it," he said. "At the very beginning, man needed to find food and protection from the elements of nature, and nalbinding offered a solution for both." So knitting was there with us right from the start; it was in our survival kit.

More recently, by spending a lot of time inside the British Library, I have managed to reconstruct the timeline and several of the details of Philippe's fascinating history of knitting. The oldest fragment of knitted textile dates to 6500 BC and was discovered in a cave in Israel. Another, dating to 4200 BC, came from a fishing village in Denmark. Was the first fragment part of a garment to shield the wearer from the heat of the Middle Eastern soil, possibly something similar to a rudimentary sock? And the second fragment, was it protecting the owner from the cold and wind of the Nordic seas? Philippe thought so.

By 1000 BC, people were nalbinding in a way that looked a lot like knitting, and they were doing it almost everywhere: in the Middle East, in Europe, in Central Asia, and in South America. Philippe was in Peru to study the hats and shawls that local tribes had knit in 300 BC.

The transition from nalbinding to knitting, using two needles instead of one, took place in the Middle East, the cradle of civilization. The motivation? Economics.

Egyptians were well-known knitters and ran a buoyant trade in knitted socks. They invented the new technique while experimenting with a faster and cheaper way to produce the socks. By AD 400, knitting had cornered the fabric market and nalbinding had disappeared. Just a few hundred years later, North African nomadic tribes were knitting using an archaic circular needle and oblong wooden frames, in which the knitting action was similar to bobbin work.

Knitting with two needles is the ancestor of the spinning jenny, the technological breakthrough that set the stage for the Industrial Revolution, I remember Philippe saying in excitement as our bus climbed the Peruvian mountains. It made production faster and cheaper, and boosted sales, so more people could afford to buy or knit their own garments. He pointed out the colorful clothes that people on the bus were wearing, most of them hand-knit. It was at that point that I fully understood what he meant when he said that knitting is the proletariat of crafts. Right from the outset, knitting has been an activity designed to meet a necessity: to feed us by helping us catch fish, to clothe us, and to protect against the heat or the cold. It has been instrumental to our survival, and because of that, it has always been an economic activity; knitted items could be bartered and even sold, so they had a value to prehistoric tribes.

Embroidery and tapestry came much later; they were not part of our survival kit and subsistence economy. These are crafts we acquired at a later stage, when we could afford to channel our creativity toward artistic production. They were primarily performed by the elite or for the elite, who could enjoy beautiful, nonessential luxuries.

"Why do you think that in *The Odyssey* Penelope weaves a shroud and does not do nalbinding?" Philippe asked me after a pause. "Because knitting was the craft of the poor, the workers, and the slaves," I replied. "You are right," he continued. "Penelope was a noblewoman. She did not knit to clothe her family—she wove beautiful shawls and shrouds to be admired. But there is another reason: nalbinding was quick, practical, and served a specific purpose. Penelope could not have spent years knitting a shroud during the day and undoing it at night—no one would have believed it."

Though knitting was an economic activity and the technique of using two needles was a major breakthrough in the craft that quickly spread across the world, European history continued to ignore knitting. "Why?" I asked Philippe. "Because the elite were indifferent to it" was his Marxist answer.

Technological innovation requires the right economic conditions to make a change, and in AD 400, the potential demand for knitted products could only have come from those who had no money to pay for them, the ancestors of the proletariat. There are plenty of these missed opportunities in history, and knitting had to wait another thousand years to become a profitable industry in Europe and to earn a place in our history books.

The first important client of precious knitted items was the Catholic Church. It acquired pillows, liturgical gloves, and other beautiful nonvital items made of imported silk and cotton, or perhaps it commissioned these luxury items in the Middle East during the Crusades. We have proof that knitting was a craft practiced in the Middle East during the first millennia. Around the same time, the church purchased exquisite knitted items from the Middle and Far East, and knitting appears in religious paintings: in 1350, a knitting Madonna was painted in Northern Italy, and later on, another was displayed in Germany. To strengthen the common belief that knitting in Europe was imported from

Islam, possibly through the Crusades, historians have pointed out that knitters cast from right to left, the same direction in which Arabic is written.

Philippe disagreed with this historical reconstruction. Peruvian tribes on the other side of the world had been knitting from right to left centuries before the birth of Islam, and nalbinding was practiced in Denmark four thousand years before Christ was born. People knit everywhere, including in the most remote places, which means the craft was one of the things men and women carried with them during the great migrations. But we have little proof of this, little evidence that they continued knitting through the centuries, because knitted fabrics generally do not last for hundreds of years.

In the British Library, I came across the story of the Faroe Islands, a small archipelago of eighteen volcanic islands in the North Atlantic, halfway between Iceland and Norway. Philippe had mentioned them during our conversation, but I could not recollect what he had told me. There is archaeological proof that people have lived in the Faroe Islands as far back as AD 300. And we know that a couple of hundred years later, Irish monks brought knitting to the islands, where wool was plentiful thanks to the vast herds of sheep. This happened before the Vikings colonized the archipelago and brought their own sheep. So several centuries before Roman cardinals fell in love with knitted cushions and gloves from the Middle East, women in the Faroe

Islands spun and knit the wool of the local sheep to clothe their families and tribes. Through the centuries, their patterns came to reproduce the striking, wild beauty of their surroundings: shades of gray, white, and charcoal constantly intertwined, evoking images of the snowy hills and cliffs of the archipelago. When the traditional Faroe Islands sweater appeared, its pattern had these colors forming a ring around the shoulders up to the neckline, just like a mountain peak. At the bottom of the sleeves, just above the wrist, and at the base of the sweater, it had an identical motif. The rest of the sweater is always of a neutral color: light gray, white, or brown. These are the colors of the archipelago's mountains through the seasons.

When our bus made a brief stop at a tiny little village a hundred miles from Cuzco, Philippe and I interrupted our conversation to get out together with the other passengers and stretch our legs. It was late afternoon and the sun was quickly disappearing behind the green mountains. I remember smelling the approaching cold dampness of the evening, which made me shiver inside my coat. Peruvians say that one special type of soft, fluffy wool from alpacas, herds of which live high up in the Andes, produces, when spun and knit, a light but solid barrier against the humidity and freezing rain of the mountains. The lanolin in this type of yarn makes raindrops slide down the fabric, keeping the wearer dry and warm. In the Northern Hemisphere, the wool of the Faroe Islands has the same characteristics and has kept its fishermen dry at sea for centuries.

Knitting is all about nature. You take one natural product—wool—spin it to transform it into a yarn, then knit it to produce fabrics that protect against the elements: rain, snow, wind, and sun. It is an exchange in which human ingenuity plays a big role: turning the raw material—wool, cotton, silk—into something that fulfills a basic need, keeping one warm or cool. Marvelously, these gifts of nature vary from place to place: wool at high altitudes, cotton along the Nile, silk in the Far East. Each satisfies the specific needs of those who inhabit that region: in the Middle East, people knit cotton to protect against the heat of the desert; in the Andes, they use alpaca wool to stay warm and dry. The one constant is our interaction with nature coupled with our creativity.

I think about Eve, about her curiosity, not about her disobedience. To seize the gifts of nature is an act of free will. It is a choice, but it is also a responsibility, one that requires a plan of action in order not to spoil it. Men and women invented spinning and knitting to produce fishing nets and fabrics to survive, and in doing so they improved the gifts of nature without destroying them. Life is also a gift of nature, and living means exercising an endless stream of acts of free will. It is a great responsibility, which involves a plan of action so as not to spoil it. Taking a wrong turn leads us off our path, but it does not necessarily ruin our life. If we are able to learn the hard lesson, we gain knowledge, we get stronger. A good knitter always treasures her mistakes; she keeps them in a special memory box that sometimes she opens to refresh her memory and wisdom. I am striving to be a good knitter, but I still have a long way to go.

A GOOD KNITTER ALWAYS TREASURES HER MISTAKES

When I was fourteen, I had a huge crush on a boy I met at the beach who was part of my *comitiva*, a big group of friends. He was two years older than me. We became a couple. After the summer, we carried on seeing each other on Saturday afternoons, but I started to get tired of him. What I thought was a great love story had turned into an embarrassment. I tried to break it off, but he did not want to, and I felt sorry for him, so I dragged out our relationship for weeks. I guess I did not know how to end it gracefully, so I behaved like a coward; I convinced myself that everything was fine.

"Knit him a sleeveless sweater," my grandmother casually suggested one day. "The curse of the sweater never fails." Most knitters are all well aware of such a curse: never knit a sweater for your boyfriend or fiancé until he becomes your husband. Knitters believe that many engagements have been broken because of this curse. Well, it worked for me. I purposely knit him a very itchy, very tight sleeveless sweater, and by the time I was done, my boyfriend had broken up with me. "See," my grandmother said with a smile when I told her I was free again, "the curse of the sweater still works. However," she added, "next time, try to be honest with yourself and simply say the truth." My grandmother was fearless—she faced life daily with a lioness's courage, like all excellent knitters.

I should have been honest with myself and my family about my marriage years ago, but instead I pretended everything was fine until catastrophe struck. Almost fifty years after the embarrassment of my failed adolescent relationship, I am facing a much, much bigger one for the same reason: my reluctance to be honest with myself. This time, the curse of the sweater would not have worked. I had to take the matter under my control, had to knit my way through financial ruin and divorce and then reinvent my life.

Back in the Andes, a shepherd walked past us and headed for the little store where the rest of the bus passengers had gone, leaving his herd in the square. The alpacas began encircling us, spitting on our shoes and making funny sounds. I could feel the warmth of their thick woolen coat on my jeans.

"Being a shepherd is one of the oldest professions," said Philippe as he stroked the alpacas' coats. "The Bible is full of stories of shepherds. And sheep have been used for milk, meat, and wool, three essential items for surviving in hostile environments." Years later, in the Iraqi desert, I understood what he meant.

In the late 1980s, I crossed the desert between al-Qaim, a vast phosphate-mining complex near the Syrian border, and Mosul, a territory that decades later was seized and subsequently lost by the Islamic State. At the time, I worked for a raw-material consultancy in London and had been asked by the Iraqi government to conduct a study on their phosphate production. My guide and driver was the export manager of the Iraqi petroleum company, which was also responsible for the phosphate mines. His name was al-Jukify.

As we headed northeast, leaving the compound that housed those who worked in the mines, al-Jukify told me that he knew the region very well because he had been born there; however, he added, only the Bedouin now lived in the desert.

For hours we traveled across a flat, stony desert with what appeared to be a fixed horizon. There was no road, no trees, no houses, no milestones. The landscape was so repetitive as to be disorienting, but my driver seemed to know where to go. At a certain point, a caravan of Bedouin surrounded by a herd of sheep appeared on the horizon. Al-Jukify explained that they were migrating from their winter pasture to their summer pasture. "Pasture?" I said. "What pasture? We are in the desert." He laughed and, pointing out at the seemingly endless stretch of dirt and stone around us, said, "There is plenty of food here for the herds." I later discovered that sheep can survive on the tiny vegetation that grows between stones and rocks, and they can go a few days without drinking water. They are the perfect domesticated animal for the subsistence economy of the nomadic Bedouin, and of our prehistoric ancestors.

Meeting strangers in the desert is a major event that must be celebrated in style, so we were invited for lunch. A tent was erected and carpets were laid inside; stools, pillows, and small tables appeared, jugs of water and yogurt were brought to us, and fires were started and food cooked. As I watched with fascination the preparation of our welcome meal, I realized that most of the tribe's possessions came from the herd. The tent was assembled with long strips of fabric woven with goat hair and sheep's wool. The women, I was told, had produced the strips and sewn them together. The curtains that divided the women's section, the private part of the tent, from the men's quarter, the public area, had been woven using camel hair. The food we ate was mutton, from the type of sheep typical of the Middle East and North Africa. The milk and yogurt we drank and cheese curds we ate also came from their sheep and goats. And the fires and stoves were fed by the animals' dung.

After our meal, I spotted a stack of knitted blankets in a corner. I asked to look at them, and the tribal leader called over a middle-aged woman, his sister, to show them to me. They were beautiful, featuring similar geometric patterns and colors to those of the tent. I thought the wool had been spun in a special way, to make the yarn thin and soft, stripping it of its thickness and most of its lanolin. These were indoor blankets. When I asked which type of wool they had used, the woman told me that it had been plucked by hand from the backs of the sheep's necks, where the texture of the wool is very fine. Years later in Unst, the most northerly of the inhabited Shetland Islands, I came across a similar technique: lace shawls, generally given as a wedding gift, are knit with wool hand-plucked from the necks of the sheep and very finely spun. The knitting stitches are so, so tiny that the entire shawl can pass through the wedding ring.

The wool I saw in Iraq was less fine but equally light. The blankets were all reversible, the geometric figures on each side the mirror image of the other side; no thread of yarn was visible. They had been knit with small needles, possibly less than 2 millimeters in diameter, and it must have taken a very long time to complete each one. I was told that the blankets were used inside the tent during the winter like big shawls, to keep the body warm. When I complimented the women who had knitted them, the tribal leader offered me one of the blankets as a gift. I was speechless.

Al-Jukify cautioned me not to decline the gift, which would have been an insult to the tribe. He suggested instead that I offer a gift in exchange. Bartering is the economic heartbeat of the Bedouin subsistence economy. I took a big silk scarf from my luggage and presented it to the tribal leader as a gift. He accepted it and passed it on to the other men sitting next to him; they all ran their hands over the scarf, enjoying the texture. The women watched from behind the camel hair curtain.

As we resumed our journey through the Iraqi desert, I asked al-Jukify if it had been hard to live in the middle of the desert, and he replied, "No, we had meat, milk, wool, and fire, and the government supplied us with books and education, what else do you need?"

Meat, milk, wool, and dung, essential products provided by herds of sheep. Our Paleolithic ancestors would probably agree with al-Jukify: What else do you need? There is a reason why the Bible is full of stories of shepherds: it is an ancient and noble profession that kept our species alive, Philippe was right. And sheep can be found almost everywhere, no matter how hostile the environment, as in Iceland or in the Faroe Islands, and they are gentle, peaceful animals.

I am told that winter in the Faroe Islands archipelago is brutal; daylight shrinks to four hours, snow is plentiful, and arctic winds batter the land at high speed. This is why the hills and mountains are bare. But like in the desert, in between the stones and turf and under the snow, there is enough food for sheep to survive and to produce meat, milk, wool, and dung to feed fires, the same basic products around which life revolves in the Iraqi desert. But in the Faroe Islands, people also have access to fish.

Some time ago I read Heðin Brú's *The Old Man and His Sons*, a celebrated tale of life in the Faroe Islands, perhaps the most popular novel of that area, featuring five essential products: meat, milk, wool, fire, and fish. The story takes place at the beginning of the twentieth century, but it is a timeless one, as life in the islands had changed very little from the previous centuries. The novel begins in summer, when a whale gets washed inside a fjord. People living up in the hills rush to sea to harvest it. Ketil, an old fisherman, is one of them, and he takes with him the last of his eleven sons, the only one still living at home.

The slaughtering of the whale is necessary but gruesome. The meat will keep starvation at bay, but seeing such a beautiful animal being mutilated is painful for everybody. Nature gives and man takes, but it does matter how we receive the gifts of nature. Nobody likes killing a whale that just hours earlier was swim-

ming free in the ocean. In the book, after the hunt, the partici-
pants are given tickets to join in the auction of the meat, which
will take place later in the day. Before the auction, Ketil meets a
friend and gets drunk, then bids too much for the meat. His son
watches in disbelief as Ketil ruins the family's finances.

When Ketil realizes what he has done, it is too late. The family will have to pay for the meat the following spring, but they do
not have enough money. If they do not find a way to repay their
bid, they will lose their house and modest possessions. So the
quest for financial help begins. The children, all married, refuse
to help; they have their own families to look after, they say, but
the real reason is that there are old feuds between Ketil's wife and
some of his daughters-in-law. Their neighbor, who they believed
was a friend, also turns them down.

Ketil and his youngest son try fishing to earn money; they
go out to sea almost every day during the summer, but the catch
is always very meager. Finally, Ketil and his wife have an idea:
They buy a great load of wool at the market, spin it, and turn it
into yarn. Ketil's wife knits it into sweaters, which they sell very
well. However, when spring comes, they realize that the profits
are insufficient to cover the debt. The book ends with the couple
selling the only cow they have after she gives birth to a calf. They
will have to wait two years before being able to milk the calf, and
without milk, there will be no cheese to sell or to eat.

We do not know what happens to Ketil and his wife; their

story is left unresolved. I like to think that they survived, and that the profits from the sale of the cow and of the knitted sweaters helped them stay afloat, just as I hope this book will provide for me. For them, as for me, knitting is the yarn of sanity, a gift of nature to stave off financial catastrophe brought upon us by our husbands' misjudgment. The yarn is the rope that prevents us from being lost at sea, and at the same time, it is also a great source of comfort.

I can picture Ketil's wife spinning and knitting day and night during the harsh and dark winter in the Faroe Islands, not in desperation but with hope, just as I can see myself reading and knitting, writing about knitting, and knitting during this winter to pay my husband's debts, and doing this with determination and hope. Ketil's wife has pushed away her daughters-in-law's mean refusal to help, just as I have not paid any attention to the indifference of my own in-laws and stepchildren about our financial needs. Amazingly, focusing on this book brings me joy and comfort in the darkest moment of my life because I love to knit and I love to write. Both heal my pain, keep me company in the solitude I have chosen to retreat into, and ease the numbness of my feelings.

Knitting is the tool Ketil's wife and I have chosen from our survival kit to heal our despair.

My yarn is still rough; it is early days for me, and my recovery is far away. But the wool is soft and fluffy, as were the coats of the alpaca herd I stroked up in the Andes decades ago. Touching it is encouraging; it gives me strength. Such beautiful wool, I think, has become a stunning yarn and will soon be a beautiful fabric. Those were the words of my grandmother before starting a new project. And indeed it did: inspired by the logo of Sleeping Beauty and her charming prince's wool business, I have knit myself a bright purple wig hat to keep me warm during my long winter (see pattern at the end of the book).

My retelling of the early history of knitting ends here, as my story, Philippe's research, and the recorded history of knitting finally merge. Around AD 1500, another major breakthrough took place: purling and stitching were invented. Knitting became smooth, elegant, and much easier. Italian merchants jumped at the opportunity to make money and began producing knitted silk stockings, which were sleek, elegant, and comfortable because they were knit without any seams. European royalty went literally crazy about them, especially men, because they could show them off while wearing short trunks, as featured in several portraits of Henry VIII.

Knitting entered high fashion, and silk stockings fueled a rich industry. During the 1500s every wealthy person in Europe, the aristocrats and royals, wore knitted garments. The knitting industry was rigorously male. Underwear, undershirts, and jackets were produced in the equivalent of sweatshops run by Italian and Spanish merchants where only men were allowed to work. However, even if the elite enjoyed wearing silk garments, knitting remained a proletariat activity, the craft of the working class, executed by exploited knitters in the workhouses of the Renaissance, enriching a new elite, the European merchants; and performed everywhere else by women to clothe their families, make ends meet, and silently create their own place in history.

Opening *the* Yarn Cage

On a May evening at a bar in West Toronto, Chris Graham, a performing artist, spoke to the audience of a monthly series called True Stories Toronto about his mother and her commitment to knitting. Born in a tiny village in Nova Scotia, Chris's mother moved to the big city, Toronto, to follow her husband, who was also a Nova Scotia native. But unlike him, she never dreamed of spending her life pursuing a brilliant career in the city. On the contrary, she probably would have been happy to stay where she was born. Chris described his mother's early life as that of a young woman from the country stuck in a noisy and chaotic city, as if she had had no choice about where and how to live.

Like so many women of her generation, Chris's mother adapted to the needs of her husband and children, never voiced her own wishes, and never complained. She looked after the house, cooked, washed their clothes. And she knit. According to her son, she was a sort of compulsive knitter, knitting any time her hands were free: on the phone, while having conversations, while watching her son play hockey or attending her daughter's ballet performances. You could picture her knitting at parties, barbecues, in movie theaters, everywhere. Naturally, she produced a phenomenal number of knitted items, far too many for just her family, so most of her "knitted output," as her son describes it, was given to charities. Together with being a wife and a mother, knitting for the community defined her. She was a true believer that you are what you can give, that you have value because of what you can contribute to others. Knitting allowed her to live by these principles.

In the Graham household, life went on for decades with Chris's father working all day in the office and coming home at night to a home-cooked meal, which would be consumed mostly in silence; the kids grew up, went to school, played sports, and did ballet, while their mother provided for them and silently knit. Life was uneventful. Then one day, she got very ill; doctors found a nasty brain cancer, diagnosed as incurable. After years of operations, chemotherapy, and radiotherapy, all of which she endured stoically, she came to the last stretch of the yarn of her life. Nobody knew how long she had, maybe several months, but surely not a full year. Throughout this ordeal, she carried on knitting.

Though she had just a few months left to live, Chris took her shopping at the yarn discount store where she had been a client since she had moved to Toronto, a three-story building that looked like a massive yarn warehouse.

Following his mother, pushing a big cart, Chris helped her choose yarn. He removed the balls of wool from the shelves, put them in the cart, having to put them back on the shelves over and over again because she kept changing her mind, deciding she preferred another color or another type of wool. She was like a child in a candy store.

You can picture the two of them inside the store, walking slowly down the aisles, flanked by walls of yarn, explosions of color all the way to the ceiling. So much to choose from! She is leading the way—this is her territory, familiar turf, and she knows all the secrets: where the best-quality wool is stocked, where the cheapest is, and where to find the most unusual yarns. Chris is behind her with the cart, following her lead inside a labyrinth of color and wool, paying attention to match her pace, ready to gather the next ball of yarn she points at.

It is a moment of special intimacy between them inside the coziness of the yarn cave. Listening to Chris's story, I got the impression that this last shopping trip was a defining event in their relationship. They both knew she was going to die soon, but they kept piling ball after ball of yarn into the cart, partners in denial. When they got to the cashier, the cart held enough yarn for her to knit for years. Chris's mother was shopping for her afterlife.

As the balls of yarn began sliding across the counter and the prices flashed across the register display, something extraordinary happened. The quiet, stoic knitter focused on the cashier, a young woman who clearly did not know her. Ignoring all the rest—her son, the cart, the walls of yarn behind her, the cascade of colors, the other customers—she announced that she was a regular customer and that Luigi, most probably the owner of the shop, always gave her a discount. So she was demanding one now.

The young woman ignored her and carried on checking out the items; she did not even look up at Chris's mother. Staring at the cashier, with the beeping sound of the checkout machine in the background, Chris's mother said that if what she had just said was not enough to get a discount, then the cashier should look at this. She took off her hat, turned her head sideways and showed the young woman the zipper of staples on her skull from all the surgeries she had endured. A dramatic gesture, a loud cry to be heard, but one that the cashier continued to ignore.

Chris was shocked—not by the fact that it was so hard to get a discount in the yarn store, or that the cashier seemed to have no heart or soul, a robot processing yarns and prices. He was taken aback by his mother's behavior. This was not the woman he had known all his life, the mother who had cooked his meals, washed his clothes, and looked after him as he was growing up, and done all this without any comment or any complaint, a silent, compulsive, almost addicted knitter. This was a woman who wanted a discount, who knew what she was entitled to have, who was expressing her needs. For the first time in his life, he was witnessing his mother demanding to be heard, calling attention to how she felt. So she did have feelings, opinions, desires, and needs, emotions that she had never verbalized, hidden instead behind the mechanics of her knitting.

How much had she suffered in silence? he wondered. Why had she never talked about herself? After her death, such self-denial was a painful burden for her children to bear. If only she had spoken to them.

Knitting had given Chris's mother comfort, it had connected her past—the rural, uneventful, and safe life she had left in Nova Scotia—with her present—the big city, an alien environment she never grew to like. Knitting had medicated her disappointment, sadness, loneliness, and longing for the life she had left behind. It had improved her new life in the city; it had helped her build the identity she had chosen: to be a giver. But at the same time, knitting had locked her inside the solitude of an existential cell, a knitted cage she had created with her own hands, a cage that had no keyhole, impossible to open from inside or out, into which not even her children had been allowed.

In the era of social media, when personal feelings and needs are shouted for all to hear, the story of Chris's mother may appear unglamorous. Though the episode at the yarn store is striking, her silent lifetime acceptance of a subordinate role vis-à-vis her husband and children could seem unremarkable. However, the opposite is true. Chris's mother's story is an excellent example of women's true power in the midst of repression at the hands of men. It shows how knitting has allowed women to play a key role in shaping society and family while being crippled by such discrimination. Chris's mother was not invisible; she was an essential presence in the household—the yarn that kept the fabric of the family growing together. And not only did she perform her duties at home, she contributed to the community. Even if she showed her true emotions only at the very end, her life had made a huge mark on those who had met and loved her.

My grandmother was right. Eve acted independently; the story of the temptation of the snake was a male trick to push her aside, to hide her free will, to make her an accessory, not a protagonist of history. Throughout the centuries, history has reenacted the same trick. Women have lived identical "silent," invisible lives while leaving their legacies behind them, unnoticed, shaping our culture, our existence, our future. History, a myopic history written by men, has passed by without paying attention to them, as if their existence was imperceptible and irrelevant. But now the knitting cage is finally opening: we have found the key, and the truth is streaming out.

Wool, spinning, weaving, and knitting have been the instruments of women's power, a testimony to their vital contribution to progress, forever. Let's grab this yarn and begin from the dawn of the new world, the birth of the American colonies, and the American War of Independence from the British Empire, and explore and unveil the truth. This is not a story passed on by my grandmother; she did not have this knowledge. This is a story I will tell.

Wool played a big role in the rising economic and commercial power of the British Empire. The textile industry was one of its biggest industries, the engine of the Industrial Revolution. Wool and cotton produced in the American colonies were exported to Great Britain at rock-bottom prices, processed and manufactured in the factories of the Midlands, and reexported back to the colonies as finished products, generating handsome profits for the British industrialists. Imagine England as a gigantic factory and the colonies as both its supplier of raw materials and its consumer market, a heavily imbalanced commercial loop that piled gold on the doorsteps of the factory owners. This economic model is known as mercantilism, a mechanism that de facto exploited the colonies for the economic benefits of the colonizers, the British merchant class.

As early as 1600, sheep from Sussex were brought to the colonies in North America. The breed was well known for producing high-quality wool and surviving on highland grasses with little nutrition. So successful was this move that in sixty years, wool production became an essential part of the economy of the colonies, to the extent that in 1664, Massachusetts passed a law requiring children to learn how to spin and weave. At a certain point, wool was more precious than tobacco. In Virginia in 1662, one yard of wool cloth was worth five pounds of tobacco. It was only a matter of time before the colonies would realize the economic power of wool production and challenge those who controlled the world market: British merchants and manufacturers. In 1699, to prevent this scenario, the British Parliament passed the Wool Act, which prohibited the colonies from exporting wool, forced them to import only British wool fabrics, and heavily taxed wool sales. It was the first of many attempts to curtail the colonies' economic growth and prevent their future independence.

The response of the American colonies was to seek self-sufficiency by boycotting British wool, a not-so-easy task. The colonies, like the rest of the British Empire, were heavily dependent upon British textiles. They did not have the industrial machinery to spin and weave, and they also lacked the commercial infrastructure and the know-how of Great Britain. But they had the wool, high-quality wool, and almost every household had a traditional spinning wheel. They also had plenty of women who knew how to spin, knit, and weave. So they challenged the highly efficient British industrial production of textile with their crafts. It was a David-and-Goliath contest.

Women took the task to heart, and did so in their usual, unglamorous way. While men openly discussed insurrection, rebellion, and even war, shouting slogans inside pubs while drinking rum, women staged spinning, weaving, and knitting competitions to produce enough textiles to allow colonists to boycott British imports. They gathered together in people's homes, in public halls, in libraries, in churches, even in outdoor squares, bringing the instruments of their crafts, and they spun, knit, and wove from sunrise to late in the evening. This homespun movement became a symbol of the colonies' disobedience toward the British Empire. People proudly wore hand-knitted and recycled clothes. It was a peaceful, powerful duel between the women of the colonies and the British manufacturers, a duel fought using the very core of the economic and commercial power of the empire as its weapon of choice: textiles.

These patriotic women came to be known as the Daughters of Liberty, the female version of the Sons of Liberty, and their gatherings were often described as "spinning bees." Indeed, the women's meetings resembled temporary hives scattered among the colonies, all of them without a queen bee; mobile craft factories where armies of women worked together like bees to keep their families and their communities alive and to build their future nation. This was a splendid example of raw democracy. Women had no right to vote and it was considered inappropriate for them to be involved in politics. But even if their voices were never recorded, even if women did not officially fight on the battlefields of the American Revolution and no woman signed the Declaration of Independence, the structure of the forthcoming democracy that the colonies had chosen in that document appears very similar to the organization and division of labor of the hives of spinning bees: a society of equals without a crowned leader, stitching and purling together to build a new nation.

In the run-up to the Revolutionary War, there is no doubt that crafts and home economics weakened the power that the British Empire exercised upon the American colonies; these were the tasks that women performed. When they were not spinning, knitting, or weaving, the women used their creativity and imagination to boycott British products in their kitchens. They raised bees to substitute honey for imported sugar, and they used spices and herbs to avoid buying British tea.

So women clothed and fed their families while saying no to British products, and in doing so they eroded the enemy's commercial lifeline and broke the mercantilism loop, paving the way for the American Revolution. When the war finally started, they were ready to clothe and feed their army.

There are so many stories of the heroism of women during the American War of Independence, carrying on performing their crucial role: crossing enemy lines to bring socks and mittens to husbands, sons, grandsons, sons-in-law, brothers, and friends; knitting blankets for the soldiers with wool recycled from sweaters, coats, and hats; smuggling bales of wool to spin in hiding and to knit and weave whatever was required at the front. Just one example is sufficient to mention: During the Siege of Boston, Sarah Bradlee Fulton, known as the mother of the Boston Tea Party, single-handedly confronted a group of soldiers who had confiscated a shipment of wool that she and her husband had bought for the sole purpose of keeping it out of the hands of the British troops. She grabbed the oxen pulling the cart full of bales of wool by the horns and reclaimed her wool. When the soldiers threatened to shoot her, she challenged them to do so. "Shoot away," she said, still holding the horns of the oxen. The soldiers did not have the courage to do so, and let her take the cart.

Women were not invisible during the American Revolution; they were essential. They fought the American War of Independence with different weapons than their men—spinning wheels, knitting needles, weaving frames, the family meal—and in doing so they contributed to the positive outcome of the revolution. But history has conveniently chosen to ignore their contribution, and when the new American nation was born on a platform of equality, women were less equal than men; they were not given the right to vote until 1920.

Like Chris's mother, the spinning bees never complained.

Their patriotism was built upon self-sacrifice, self-discipline, and personal piety; they did not seek power, and they did not even demand recognition for their heroism. Their role was to look after their families, and since independence from the British Empire meant improving the lives of their families, achieving freedom was synonymous with prosperity for the household. Women took the textile challenge upon their shoulders for their loved ones, not to seek political power (we had to wait for the suffragettes to hear the first real female political cry). Like Chris's mother, these women refrained from expressing their needs and true feelings; they remained silent and unmentioned in history, but they did change the course of history, just as Eve's curiosity and act of free will altered the future of humanity. Like Chris's mother, the legacy of all these women is stronger than ever.

The American War of Independence was not the only war women fought with the instruments of their craft. Women have knitted for the soldiers, the wounded, the refugees during all conflicts: the Crimean War, the Boer War, and, as my grandmother did, World War I.

Many years ago, I met a very interesting woman who was born in the same year as my grandmother, 1900. Her name was Gladys. She lived in a council estate (a British public housing complex) in Battersea, in London. I had asked the owner of Honor Parry, my local wool shop, to find someone who could knit a woolen blanket for me using a pattern I had come across in the Lake District. Honor Parry's owner—a lovely old-fashioned English lady who proudly lived above the shop with her husband in an apartment without central heating—chose Gladys because Gladys was a good and attentive knitter, "even if she was in her nineties," she said. The pattern was not too difficult but required constant arithmetic to reproduce its geometric design. One evening I received a call: Gladys had run out of yarn and was just about to finish the blanket, did I have an extra ball? Luckily, I did, and offered to take it to her right away.

The council estate where Gladys lived was just two blocks from my house, but the social distance between our residences was as vast as an ocean. I lived in a big house facing Battersea Park, in the so-called posh area; she lived two roads south of the park, in public housing.

Gladys lived in a pristine one-bedroom flat with lace curtains on the windows, a comfortable sofa, and the soft smell of lavender. I never knew how she had ended up living there—she never told me, and the owner of the wool shop did not know, either—but that evening, Gladys did tell me that she lived alone, that her husband had died many years earlier, and that she had no children or relatives; she was all alone in the world. "But," she added, "I am perfectly all right. I enjoy being in charge of my life, and I have my knitting to keep me busy."

I gave her the ball of wool, and she offered to show me the blanket over a cup of tea. I accepted, and while she went into the kitchen to make the tea, I looked at the blanket. It was magnificent. The stitches were even, linked together by a steady hand. The geometric pattern was visible at first glance and it was perfect; my eyes ran over it, intrigued and pleased by its complexity. I glanced at her knitting bag, neatly resting on the side of an armchair facing the TV. Inside was all the equipment of a good knitter, including the ball of wool I had just given her.

When Gladys came back, she was holding only one cup of tea. It was for me, she explained; she never drank tea after four p.m. As she handed me the cup, she took the blanket from my hands, sat in the armchair, grabbed the new ball of wool from the bag, and began knitting.

"If you can wait half an hour, I can finish the blanket and you can take it home with you," she said. There was something special about her, I thought, as I sipped the tea and watch her knitting, an aura of youth, an ageless glow. She was in her nineties but she looked much younger.

We started talking about knitting. Gladys had knit all her life, professionally for more than thirty years, she said; she had also knit for designers and boutiques, but recently it had become more and more difficult to get work. I nodded and added that we were in the middle of the biggest recession since the oil shock in the 1970s. She smiled and said that the current economic crisis was nothing in comparison to the war. It was a sentence that could easily have come from my grandmother's lips.

I began talking about my grandmother, how much I missed her. She had died just a year earlier, and I was still struggling with the idea that I would never talk to her again. When I told Gladys that my grandmother had fallen in love with my grandfather while knitting socks for him during World War I, her eyes lit up. Gladys had also knit socks for her father and brothers at the front.

When the war started, she said, people volunteered to fight; that was what men did at that time. All the men in her family had gone to war and the women had been left behind. "We lived in a farm in Sussex," she recalled. "It was not ours; we rented it. I remember my mother crying quietly in the kitchen after everybody had gone. She was worried about running the farm alone, with only the help of us girls. She was worried about paying the rent. But we managed, somehow we did, not because the government helped us, but because we all pulled together, the village, the town, the county. Mostly women, as the men had all gone to the front. We were lucky: our landlord was a patriot, he had also volunteered, and his wife never bothered us. We paid the rent when we could."

As she talked, I observed her knitting. She was not especially fast, but the stitches were firm and she looked very much in control. She used long metal needles, like my grandmother had, the type that is common in Scotland but not in the southeast of England. Gladys held the yarn with determination and the needles carried it along with incredible grace. I noticed that she had long, beautiful, manicured hands, not disfigured by arthritis; her skin was still very white with only a few age spots. She was also wearing red nail polish, the type in fashion in the 1950s, something that I thought very extravagant. As she knit, her red fingernails seemed to perform an exotic dance against the background of the creamy wool.

"World War One was a shock for all of us," Gladys went on. "As the first letters arrived from the front, we discovered that soldiers did not have enough equipment and they lacked proper clothes. I guess this must have been true before also, during the previous wars, but we did not expect the mighty British government to send our men to the trenches without enough socks, not in the twentieth century. When we read about trench foot, a fungus that attacked the feet of the soldiers because they were always wet in the trenches, we were horrified. As soon as we were told that the only way to prevent it was to change socks very often, to make sure both the socks and the feet were always dry, we acted. Our men at the front needed socks, lots of socks, and we were going to supply them.

"And so we began knitting; every spare moment, we knit.

Everyone who was not at the front was knitting. The train conductor while in the station, the secretaries on their lunch hour, the shopkeepers when there were no clients, commuters traveling on trains and buses. It was a spontaneous effort. At the beginning, no one told us to knit—we took the initiative because we cared. We knit with whatever wool we had: we unraveled sweaters, blankets, scarfs, hats, anything we could get our hands on that could be spared became a ball of wool. We worked out how much of each color we had and designed a pattern; we wanted these garments, which we called comfort goods, to be warm but also to look good, red-and-blue-striped socks, yellow-and-brown balaclavas, black-and-white vests."

Did the men recognize the wool? Did they remember the old items the new things came from, and which member of the family had worn them? Of course they did. The recycled yarns kept them closer to home, connected to their loved ones; it was an endless yarn of love.

I remember my grandmother telling me that on the rare occasions on which my grandfather talked of the trenches, he always mentioned the absence of color. Everything was gray. The grass had died, the trees and bushes had been burned, insects had flown away. I can imagine him opening a package from my grandmother in such a bleak landscape and being hit by the flash of colors of her socks. Red, green, blue, white, and yellow, real colors, like those in the rainbow, beautiful colors. And I can imagine him clinging to those colorful garments, testimony that there was another life to live, that he had had another life, that the war, the trenches, and the colorless landscape that surrounded him would eventually go away; all he needed to do was stay alive long enough to get back to that life.

"The government did not like our spontaneous knitting," Gladys confessed. "It particularly disapproved of the colors because it exposed its lack of preparation for the war, its inability to provide proper clothing for the soldiers. Imagine an army marching with exotic and colorful socks, gloves, vests, and caps under their helmets!"

I heard her voice and suddenly realized that what she was saying was very unusual. British people of her age, especially those

who survived the war, do not talk like that to strangers or criticize authority so openly. I wondered if she was a communist, or maybe just an eccentric. I later discovered from the owner of the wool shop that she had been involved in politics, which had caused several problems in her life, including a sudden dismissal from a prominent boarding school where she was a teacher. I wish I had asked her more about her political views that evening. Gladys died in her sleep a few weeks after my visit. My magnificent blanket was among the last items she knitted.

During my recent research on knitting, I came across the work of a British scholar, Jane Tynan, who confirmed what Gladys had told me thirty years ago about the British government's lack of preparation for war and about how the colorful items knitted at home clashed with the disciplined look of the soldiers' uniforms. Just as Gladys had surmised, if an army marches with yellow-and-red socks, light blue balaclavas, and striped scarves, it does not appear to some to be a serious and well-funded army. Professor Tynan also talks about how spontaneous knitting by women back at home became a worldwide phenomenon. No government engaged in the war was well equipped for it, so socks and other clothing were needed everywhere, to keep the soldiers warm on both sides of the trenches. German women also knit in Technicolor for their loved ones, unraveling whatever knitted items they could get their hands on and spare.

So women and those who were not actively fighting contributed to the war effort by knitting. They did it without a military or state structure, spontaneously, just like the knitting bees of the American Revolution. Knitting was once again part of a grassroots movement, but because of that, it represented a threat to the British government during World War I. At the beginning of the twentieth century, the state, any state, saw a strong anarchist component in any grassroots movement, something that could not be controlled, something that could turn into opposition against the establishment. Women constituted the great majority of the spontaneous knitting movement, and in many countries, women still did not have the right to vote, so there was an additional element of potential subversion in knitting freely, without a state or military structure in command to supply wool and patterns. Spontaneous knitting had the strength to rattle the yarn cage and to challenge the status quo, and the British government, like many others, was afraid it would break open, exposing the injustice of gender segregation.

Jane Tynan believes that one of the responses of the British government to the spontaneous knitting of the women during World War I was the so-called Kitchener stitch, a way to knit socks using four needles without seams that would chafe the soldiers' skin. Herbert Kitchener was the British secretary of state for war at the time, and a new sock pattern he wrote brought the spontaneous knitting frenzy under the control of the Crown. Women were given strict instructions: they had to follow a specific pattern, distributed by the government; they were told which type of wool to use and in what colors—dark green and gray, to match the soldiers' uniforms (see pattern at the end of the book). The knitters could not have any imagination or creativity; they were mere accessories of the war machine. The yarn cage got a new lock, but its bars were rusting. It was only a matter of time before it would collapse.

CHAPTER THREE

Knitting *for* *the* Revolution

When you knit, the yarn dances around the needles, my grandmother told me; there is a rhythm, a melody that flows from your head to your fingers. The pattern is the sheet of music and the knitter has to orchestrate the composition. A shawl can be loosely or tightly knit, depending on the way one wants it to be or plans to use it. It can be dressy or warm, elegant or functional. Choosing the type of yarn and the colors is part of the choreography of the knitting ballet and must be in tune with the type of garment one wants to produce.

A good knitter has a vision of the finished product before she starts, just as a conductor and a choreographer have a vision of the composer's work they want to stage. A good knitter knows how to read a pattern by simply glancing at a knitted item. She can look at a garment in a shop window and see the dance, the choreographed sequences of stitches, encoded in it.

I discovered the true language of knitting when I was reading *A Tale of Two Cities* by Charles Dickens. I was ten or eleven years old at the time, and I had been knitting for a few years. My father had bought me a collection of classic books, which I devoured and discussed with my grandmother as we knitted together. She had read them all, remembered all the stories, and had so many insights about both the facts and the fiction.

"This woman, Madame Defarge," my grandmother said to me one day as she knit a bedcover for her goddaughter's wedding. "Do you really believe she existed and encoded in her knitting the names of the aristocrats who were beheaded?" Of course I believed it—Charles Dickens, one of my favorite authors, had said it was so! My grandmother shook her head. "To what purpose?" she continued. "For revenge," I said, "because the French aristocracy had oppressed the people for so long, had abused its powers, and the Revolution brought justice to the masses."

"Madame Defarge is a fictional character created to symbolize the brutality of the Revolution, of any revolution, through the dehumanization of those involved in it," my grandmother said. "It does not tell you the real story of the tricoteuses, the Frenchwomen who sat and knit in front of the guillotine." *Wow,* I thought in excitement, *there is more to the story than I have read.*

And so she began one of her master history lessons.

In the second half of the eighteenth century, she told me, market women in Paris were the backbone of society. They worked, traded, administered their husbands' meager salaries, looked after the kids, clothed their families with their knitting and sewing, and made ends meet. They were the barometers of social stability. When they realized they had no more bread to feed their families, they rebelled. They marched on Versailles, demanding bread because they were hungry. That was the spark that started the French Revolution.

Years later, while taking a course on the French Revolution at university, I discovered that those women had become heroines in the people's eyes. They created groups, presided over by women such as Reine Audu, Agnès Lefevre, Marie Louise Bouju, and Rose Lacombe, similar to the Jacobin Club, which was one of the most radical movements of the Revolution, headed by Robespierre. These courageous women walked the streets of Paris insulting whoever they thought was wealthy and encouraging the revolutionaries to arrest them. They were invited to observe the National Convention, the first assembly to govern France during the Revolution, which formally abolished the monarchy.

My grandmother continued the knitting history lesson. Soon, she said, the revolutionary government felt threatened by these women, by their political role, rising power, and popularity within the Revolution. The market women may have been the spark of the Revolution, but its management was firmly in the hands of men, men who became increasingly authoritarian. So it was decided that the women could not sit in the gallery during meetings of the National Convention, and eventually they were forbidden to participate in any political assembly. But the women did not give up on being part of this process they had started. Some of them moved to the Place de la Révolution (today known as the Place de la Concorde), where the executions took place. They brought chairs from their market stalls and miserable homes and placed them around the guillotine, then sat all day watching their enemies getting their heads severed from their bodies. And they brought their knitting.

The revolutionary government was helpless to stop them. The square was a public place, and people were encouraged to witness the executions, so no one could ask the market women to move. Being accustomed to trade, the women started to sell their seats to people who wanted to watch the executions of specific individuals. They also knit various garments, socks, mittens, and scarfs, which they sold after the executions. But mostly they knit the red *bonnets de la Liberté* ("Liberty caps") that became one of the symbols of the French Revolution, worn by everyone in Paris. Renting the chairs and selling the items they knit proved to be a good business for the market women, even more profitable than their traditional trade. This was a blessing, because during the Revolution, it was harder for people to make even a meager living. Remarkably, the market women were able to support their families with their knitting.

The Liberty cap, I discovered in school, is a copy of an ancient hat, the Phrygian cap, which originated in Anatolia. Marianne, the symbolic figure who embodies "liberty, equality, and fraternity"—the motto of the French Revolution—is always depicted as wearing a red Phrygian cap (see pattern at the end of the book).

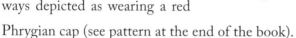

As usual, my grandmother's interpretation of historical events, especially when knitting was involved, had a unique twist. Dickens wrote that the market women knit as a substitute for eating and drinking, a totally nonsensical conclusion, according to her. When you are almost starving, as the people of Paris were at the end of the eighteenth century, nothing can replace a loaf of bread, not even knitting.

I must confess that as a child, I found the idea that the tricoteuses knit while watching people die deeply disturbing. Associating knitting with a violent act was not possible; it did not make any sense. It was my grandmother who explained to me why knitting came to be linked with the beheading of the French aristocrats. The market women knit during meetings of the assembly, she said, and they knit as the heads of the aristocrats rolled into the basket at their feet all for a simple reason: they always knit. Knitting was a part of their lives, just like breathing and working; it was a required activity. The tricoteuses had to keep busy all the time. Even when they were entertaining themselves with their revenge over the aristocrats, they had to be productive. "And by the way," she added, "none of them knew how to read or write." So they could not have encoded the names of the executed aristocrats in their knitting, as Dickens claimed they had.

My grandmother was brought up in a similar fashion, raised to be constantly productive. She was the first daughter of twelve children. Her mother died in childbirth when my grandmother was ten, and her father remarried her aunt, her mother's sister, and had another six children. Though the family was modestly wealthy, my grandmother looked after her brothers and sisters, sewed and knitted most of their clothes, and helped her mother and then her stepmother to run the household. Every day she woke up at four thirty in the morning and attended to her daily tasks before going to school. Reading was her only pleasure; at the end of the day, when she had finished her work, she sat in the kitchen losing herself in any book she could get ahold of.

"Dickens was right in one thing," she said. "Knitting is a language that only knitters understand. You can knit anything into your pattern: a name, a story, a prayer, or a poem." Then she showed me how she had knit her wisdom about marriage into the wedding blanket she was making for her goddaughter. She took my finger and guided it over the purls and stitches in a corner of the blanket and read out the words hidden there: "*Love is a daily victory and a lifetime treasure.*"

Have I failed to follow her guidance, to live according to those knitted words I felt underneath my fingers as a child? As my mind goes back to those magic years of wool, yarn, needles, storytelling, and history and compares them with my present anguish, I can see many holes in the pattern of my life. I have done my best to keep that life's treasure safe, but I have failed. Is it my fault? Sometimes love vanishes for reasons beyond our control, and sometimes life plays nasty tricks on us. One spring morning, my grandmother kissed her beloved husband and wished him a good day on his way to work; a few hours later, his heart stopped and hers broke. But she carried on; somehow, she did. I am at a similar junction: my husband, my caring, loving companion of more than thirty years, has vanished, and my heart is broken, but I must carry on. As in the very, very difficult sequence of the stitches of war, I cannot give up, I cannot skip one single move, I have to tackle each one with courage and determination until I reach the end.

Courage, I need it so desperately. The same courage of the knitting spies, the men and women who during two World Wars spied for the Allies using knitting as their covert messaging system.

Knitting is ideal for hiding messages, like Morse code, because it is binary: there are only two stitches, knit and purl. Positions of troops, numbers of weapons, movements of trains—everything can be hidden in a simple hat, in a pair of mittens, in a scarf. For the non-knitter, it is impossible to read the codes; even knitting patterns themselves appear to be written in a secret code. This explains why during World War II, the British government banned all printed knitting patterns out of fear that they could be used to communicate information to the Germans.

British intelligence made great use of their knitting spies, but so did the Germans. Unverified reports published in the 1940s in the British periodical *Pearson's Magazine* claimed that German spies knit entire sweaters with yarn full of knots, which, once unraveled and placed in a frame containing the letters of the alphabet, revealed secret messages. But the most exciting true stories of knitting spies come from occupied Europe during the two World Wars.

During World War I, in Roubaix, near Lille, a region of France under German occupation, Madame Levengle, a woman who lived in a house overlooking the loading yard of the Roubaix railway station, was a knitting spy. Louise de Bettignies, a truly remarkable woman, had recruited Levengle into the Alice Network, a group of spies and allies who operated in Northern France, Belgium, and the Netherlands, gathering and passing on intelligence about the Germans to the British. Madame Levengle sat knitting in front of a window on the first floor of her house overlooking the loading yard. Each time she saw something to report, she tapped out the information on the floor in code. Her children, pretending to do their homework on the floor below, wrote down the codes. To understand the courage of this woman and her children, one has also to know that they did this dangerous work even as a German field marshal lived in their home.

During World War II, the Belgian Resistance enrolled older women who, like Madame Levengle, lived near train lines and loading yards and could watch the German movements as they knit. These women reported messages in their knitting using codes that were rather simple but very effective: a dropped stitch, which produced a hole, for example, signified the passing of one type of train; purling on a field of knit stitches, which forms a bump in the fabric, referred to another type of train. The finished knitted fabrics were then handed over to fellow spies in the Belgian Resistance.

Although both sides used knitting spies, knitting proved to be an excellent cover for those spying for the Allies. Elizabeth Bentley, an American, carried clandestine material from the US government to Soviet agents inside her knitting bag. She hid microfilms, memos, and coded documents in a basket full of balls of wool, needles, patterns, and fabric. After the war, when people referred to her as the "Red Spy Queen," she replied that a better name would have been the "Communist June Cleaver"—the ultimate dutiful housewife character of the popular 1950s show. The absurdity of this image illustrates why knitting was such a successful cover: in the collective imagination of the first half of the twentieth century, a woman knitting was the antithesis of a spy.

Phyllis "Pippa" Latour Doyle was one of the knitting spies who proved this stereotype wrong. Her amazing life story could easily have come from my grandmother's lips. It is a hidden gem from a time of heroism, self-sacrifice, and courage, but it also is a testimony to the modesty of those who were motivated by a strong sense of duty and honor to fight Nazism. Pippa did not reveal her spying activity to anyone, keeping it secret even from her own children, until several decades after the war ended. Only then was her heroism praised and her story published in the *New Zealand Herald*. One of the forty women members of the Special Operations Executive, the secret force that Winston Churchill wanted to use to "set Europe ablaze," her code name was Genevieve.

At the age of twenty-three, Latour, perfectly fluent in French, was trained to become a British spy inside occupied France. On a cold winter night, she was parachuted into the darkness of war, behind enemy lines, with her precious communication code encrypted in a length of silk yarn that she wore as a ribbon in her hair.

Genevieve cycled across occupied France, reporting on the position and movements of the Germans, carrying her knitting in her basket. She recorded her discoveries, purling and stitching in the coded message and then transmitting the information via radio from different locations. A few times she was stopped and searched by the Germans and narrowly escaped being discovered. Once, a female police officer asked her to strip naked on the suspicion that she was hiding something underneath her clothes. The officer even untied the silk yarn that held her hair back, and Pippa shook her head to prove that there was nothing hidden in her hair.

Knitting for the Revolution, knitting for the resistance, knitting for spying: the stories I learned through my childhood, adolescence, and youth have all enriched my life, and I like to think that they helped me become a better adult and have guided me through my present ordeal. My grandmother was my first guru, but she was not the only one.

In 1985, I moved with my first husband to San Francisco. We arrived a week before Halloween, and the entire city was in costume. The cashier at the bank was dressed as Dracula, the waiter at the small restaurant across from the hotel where we stayed was wearing a Frankenstein's monster outfit, and the landlord of the apartment we wanted to rent looked like John Lennon after he came back from India. He wore a pair of white bell bottoms, two sizes too big; a loose Afghan shirt, also white; and a long, hand-knit tie-dyed vest that almost reached the floor. He had long light brown hair parted in the middle of his forehead and a bushy beard down to his chest, and looked at me from behind a pair of small, perfectly round glasses. When he opened the door to the apartment, for a split second I thought I was time-traveling. I could hear the beautiful voice of Grace Slick, accompanied by Jefferson Airplane, singing "White Rabbit," smell the marijuana he was smoking, and feel the waves of peace and love washing over the rugs and colorful cushions scattered on the floor of his sitting room. Could it be possible that the clock had stopped in 1967, the year of the summer of love?

Greg, our landlord, was not wearing a costume. He was a hippie, one of the last still standing. He had lived all his life two blocks from the corner of Haight and Ashbury Streets, the epicenter of the summer of love. He was a Deadhead, a fan of the Grateful Dead, who also lived in the Bay Area. He went to all their concerts and remembered them well (I never understood how, as Greg's memory was often patchy due to his extensive usage of LSD and other drugs). He did not work—he did not need to, because he had inherited two houses near Golden Gate Park that he rented out and an apartment in Haight-Ashbury, the one we eventually rented for the two years we spent in San Francisco. Apart from music and drugs, he loved knitting. And so we bonded, purling and stitching in his colorful and timeless living room.

The hippie generation was the first generation that rejected everything their parents stood for. They refused to go to war, they objected to working nine to five, and they did not cut their hair. They wanted free love, not marriage, and they experimented with drugs. They were gentle rebels, nonviolent and peaceful, and loved knitting. They believed that manufacturing your own clothes was a strong anticapitalist statement, and that knitting skirts, sweaters, vests, hats, socks, and all the necessary accessories, from handbags to belts, was a revolutionary act against Western consumerism.

Greg had learned how to knit at an outdoor concert in Golden Gate Park during the summer of love. A couple had settled on the grass near him and started knitting. A few people gathered around them, watching what they were doing, and those sitting next to them were handed needles and yarn. Greg decided to join them and was taught how to purl and stitch. And that was it—he was hooked for life.

Perhaps it was the drugs, he told me, or the music, or the colors of the yarns, who knows? "But the moment I understood how to purl and stitch," Greg said, "when I saw the yarn move like a snake along the needle, I fell in love with knitting as I had fallen in love with rock and roll when I heard Elvis for the first time.

"The first garment I knitted was a striped vest," he went on. "I got the yarn from a shop in Chinatown. They were selling bags of wool of different colors by the weight. I wore the vest to a concert, and friends came up to me asking where I had gotten it. When I said I had knitted it, they asked me to knit some for them. I began knitting professionally; I sold my creations, all vests, at concerts and festivals. I always knitted two identical garments, one for men and one for women. Many couples at the time liked to wear the same outfit. It was a way to tell everyone they were in love." (See pattern at the end of the book.)

In the 1970s, knitted vests were hot, hot, hot, and most of them were unisex. London was the epicenter of the European hippie knitting fashion; Jean Machine in King's Road, Biba in Kensington, and Carnaby Street were some of the boutiques to visit. The first time I went to London in 1971, I was sixteen years old, and I went on a knitting pilgrimage. At the time there were no smartphones, and you could not go into a shop and take a picture of an outfit with your camera, so I had to memorize the amazing merchandise I could not afford to buy. There were knitted vests everywhere, and I wanted to copy them all. I studied the stitches and the patterns, ran them through my mind a few times, then transcribed the information into a notebook.

When I got back home, I went to see my grandmother. I described to her what I thought was the most beautiful knitted garment I had ever seen, a soft, slightly shiny black lace chenille vest. The lace was complicated because it had no repetition; it consisted of several geometrical figures, almost randomly knit, but reading the pattern showed a logic, a harmony in the position of the figures. The small ones floated in the middle of the big ones, a trick to make the fabric look almost 3D. I showed my grandmother a drawing of the lace I had made and one of the shape of the vest, which had long fringe at the bottom. Could she help me knit it? Of course she would, but without the fringe, I was not an Indian squaw, she said, to my embarrassment. My grandmother did not like the hippies; she thought they were spoiled brats and she found their fashion outrageous, especially the ethnic clothing, but she was a super-knitter and loved a challenge, and the lace chenille vest was one of those. But above all, she loved me.

I was crazy about hippie fashion; I thought it was an expression of freedom, original and personal. It was revolutionary. Even today, when I see pictures from those years I feel a pang in my heart: that was a time in which everything was about freedom of expression through life, including clothes—not via Twitter, Facebook, Instagram, or social media in general.

Greg had remained loyal to hippie fashion and to the philosophy behind it. He dressed in traditional clothing from India, the hippies' favorite style. It was a statement against the establishment that had almost sent him to war in Vietnam.

One evening, while we were knitting as we watched reruns of *Dallas* on TV, he told me what had happened to him during the Vietnam War. "My family and I were sitting in front of the television," he said, "listening to the birth dates with low draft numbers, and suddenly there it was, the day and the year I was born. I was going to war! No one could say a word; we looked at each other, unable to comprehend what had happened. Then my mother started crying and my father did not know what to do, console her or comfort me. He stood in the middle of the room, hopeless. Luckily, the examiners found an irregularity in my heartbeat and I never did go to Vietnam.

"I lost several friends in that absurd war, young, beautiful, happy, and unlucky men," said Greg. "To remember them, I knitted a blanket with their names, and when I feel down, I take it out and wrap it around me to remember the gift of life that was handed to me. I still do not understand the meaning of the Vietnam War. I get the politics, the Cold War, et cetera, but I do not see the logic of several American presidents sending all those boys to be slaughtered. Why did they not stop the war sooner? It is like a bad knitter who continues knitting, knowing that he has made a major mistake, a structural mistake, too many stitches at the beginning, or too few, and the shape of what he is knitting is wrong. It will never fit, it will never work, he knows he is wasting time and yarn, but he carries on regardless."

Courage. What the bad knitter lacks is the courage to admit he has made a major mistake and has to start from the beginning. Kennedy, Johnson, and Nixon were definitely bad knitters.

Unraveling all the knitting, letting it go, pulling out the yarn, and undoing stitch after stitch in order to start again from the beginning, is painful. And as you undo your fabric, you watch hours and hours of work unspool, rewinding and ending up with a ball of twisted yarn, injured wool. Yes, it is excruciatingly painful. But sometimes it has to be done.

When we lived in San Francisco, I lost a baby. I had a miscarriage at the end of my first trimester. I knew on my way to the hospital that my baby would never be born. I felt the contractions undoing the fetus, unraveling my pregnancy. I also knew that by the time I left the hospital, nothing would be left inside me; my baby would be gone forever.

A week later, Greg came to visit me at home. I was putting away a pile of knitting clothes and blankets intended for the baby, and yes, I was crying. He took my hand and made me sit on the couch.

"Think about having your favorite hand-knitted cashmere

cardigan washed in the machine at ninety degrees," he said. "What comes out is a bundle of thick, rough wool. It is unusable. Your beloved cardigan is gone and the wool cannot be salvaged; it is a total loss. You feel shocked, infuriated, sad, and responsible, because you should have protected that cardigan, made sure it was not going to end up inside the washing machine. But you are a knitter, a good knitter, and can knit another cardigan. It is not going to be the one you lost, but another one, perhaps even more beautiful that the first one."

I am a knitter, not a great one, but a decent one, and yes, I can knit another cardigan, I thought. *I can and will have another baby.*

The last time I spoke with Greg was in the summer of 2002. He had just come back from the Global Knit-In at the G8 summit, held that year at the remote Kananaskis Resort, a ninety-minute drive from Calgary, in Alberta, Canada. He told me he was leaving San Francisco. Silicon Valley had destroyed the magic of the city, and he was relocating to India. But before abandoning America for good, he had answered the call to action of the Revolutionary Knitting Circle, a protest group born in Calgary in 2000. He was enthusiastic about the initiative, part of craftivism, a global antiestablishment movement. However, he felt the yarn of his life was taking him somewhere else, to the villages of Kashmir. When I told him I had never heard of craftivism, he was shocked. Where was I living? Was I not hooked on the global knitting network? Did I not notice that a major knitting renaissance was underway?

Knitting as a political tool to challenge the dark side of globalization, from income inequalities to the implosion of social democracy, is one of the best-kept secrets of our time. Somehow, the establishment managed to convince the media that knitting as a political protest is limited to a very small number of eccentric, nutty activists. But the opposite is true. Knitting as a political protest has grown exponentially since the beginning of the twenty-first century, and those who have joined the protest have a clear vision of what is wrong in our society. Their rhetoric is often revolutionary, at times even reminiscent of Marxism. Their aim is to empower the disenfranchised peacefully, through knitting. It is not just a pet project of millennials, posting pictures of blankets knitted for trees on Instagram. It is a peaceful and powerful statement about the disintegration of our society, the destruction of the environment, and the implosion of social values—all in the name of greed.

After my conversation with Greg, I came across the call to action of the Revolutionary Knitting Circle for the Global Knit-In, which states: "The G8 claims to be a gathering of democratic leaders. The Revolutionary Knitting Circle proclaims that they are anything but. The G8 is a meeting of the wealthiest of the world to decide the fates of the vast majority of the world who are in no way represented by these 'leaders.'" I could not agree more, and I would add to the G8 all the other international initiatives, from the G20 to the International Monetary Fund (IMF) and the World Bank. What have they done to promote justice, democracy, and equality, to fight poverty, crime, and hunger, to prevent war, help refugees, and save our planet? I leave the answer to the reader.

The magic of San Francisco is gone, Greg is right, and our world has deteriorated. But the yarn of life that stretches across the Golden Gate Bridge has not been cut. The global knitting movement is living proof of this. On the contrary: the yarn of life is as strong and solid as it was in the summer of 1967. All we need to do is to find it in the heaps of products and apps that pile up daily in our lives.

Yes, we live in hard times, and once again, war is the pattern we are knitting, a complicated, almost incomprehensible series of stitches that scares even the best knitter. A pattern of an elusive war, because it is not on our doorstep but inside our souls. And

once again, we need courage and determination to get through it, one stitch at a time, until we get to the end. Modern knitters have it, I discovered while researching and writing this book.

Perhaps the world is unaware of the contemporary global knitting revolution because the media have been presenting political knitting as the artistic expression of a few talented artists. But behind these remarkable artists, there are millions of people who share their protest and their understanding of the power of knitting. They knit alone or in groups, stitching together a fractured world, mending the holes politicians are opening daily, purling and stitching as fast as they can to get us to the end of the war pattern so that we can start knitting the fabric of peace once again.

In 2006, Danish artist Marianne Jørgensen knit a pink tea cozy over a combat tank to protest her country's involvement in the Iraq War. In 2005, Lisa Anne Auerbach produced "body count mittens," numbered with the Iraq War death toll; the bodies kept piling up so fast that the second mitten of a pair would have a higher number than the first. Knitters like these are the vanguard of the global political knitting movement, but to understand them, one must recognize that knitting is often much more than an isolated, individual pastime; in fact, it is a force that brings people together for the greater good. That is the power of knitting.

CHAPTER FOUR

Feminism's Love-Hate Relationship *with* Yarn

W hile I am writing this book, I also have to deal with my personal crisis. To avoid financial ruin, I have to put in place various financial schemes to stay afloat until I can liquidate my biggest asset, a house in a glitzy American ski resort. To make this strategy work, I had to mortgage my home in London and then rent it to cover the monthly payments.

While I was packing up my office, I came across a very old photo. In it, it is winter, and I must be six or seven years old. I am at the bottom of a ski slope, and right behind me I can see my father. We must have just skied down the mountain. I am sucking on a handful of snow; I remember sometimes doing this when I was thirsty while skiing. Because of the incline of the slope, the photo shows my father's chest right behind my head. I have looked at this black-and-white picture millions of times, but today, for the first time, I notice that it is remarkably similar to one of the knitting ads I had recently seen in 1960s women's magazines while researching this book.

I remember that day. It was a sunny midwinter day, and we were skiing at Terminillo, a ski resort near Rome. My father and I wore identical Nordic sweaters, dark blue with white motifs of reindeers and snowflakes circling our shoulders. My grandmother had knit my father's and my mother had knit mine. They had done this in secret, to surprise us before our ski trip. That very morning, my father and I had woken up, put on our identical sweaters, and gone to breakfast, father and daughter proudly wearing matching ski outfits.

I have kept that framed photo on one of the shelves in my office for decades because I have always associated that day with a happy time in my life, a time long gone, when my father and I went skiing together and my mother and grandmother stayed at home, looking after my younger brother, taking care of the house, cooking our meals, and, yes, knitting for us. As a child, I never wondered why my mother did not join us, why my father spent his winter weekends skiing with me, a little girl, while his wife was engaged in domestic activities. I was brought up inside the traditional female-male gender divide yet unaware of my true nature. My father raised me as a boy; I was physically fit, fearless, quick to learn, and would have followed him to the center of the earth if he had asked. I looked at my mother and at the world in general with male eyes, with my father's eyes. I did not know that my mother and I belonged to the same sex and that, most likely, after puberty, I would share her destiny.

In post–World War II Western society, women were predominantly housewives, men went to work to provide for the family, and everybody was a consumer. The picture-perfect married couple was a social portrait that from an economic point of view made a lot of sense: Men had come back from the war and needed jobs; women, who had kept the economy going while the men were gone, had to return to the home. They could not compete with their husbands on the job market; their tasks were to bear children and look after their families. Modern capitalism demanded this division of labor because it was believed to be the fastest avenue to repopulate war-torn nations, countries that would soon become buoyant consumer markets, outlets for production.

From a social point of view, no one could object to the housewife–working husband paradigm because it reproposed, in a modern key, the traditional separation between female and male roles. Historically, too, the return to normality after periods of great political upheaval had always been accompanied by the reinforcement of the classic gender division of labor. And women had accepted this transition: after the American War of Independence, for example, women who had made those events possible with their craft and skills willingly marched back into the yarn cage, letting men claim all the victory. In 1945, therefore, it made sense economically and socially to believe that after the madness of war and destruction, reentrenching this gender stereotype guaranteed peace and economic stability, and provided a comforting social cocoon for future generations.

In the late 1940s, no one was expecting women to rebel. And indeed, for over a decade, it seemed that women were happy to be confined to marriage and the home. Through the 1950s, marriage became the primary aspiration of young Western women. In the United States, for example, women's average age for marrying dropped to twenty, and the number of women going to college went down considerably. Women seemed eager to lock themselves into the marital home, to become housewives and mothers and look after their families. However, unlike in the past, these women were more than wives and mothers: they were also consumers. In a society where economic growth was intimately linked to consumption, women, who represented more than half the population, could not be kept out of the market.

Paradoxically, modern capitalism, which shunned women in the labor force, had, without knowing it, handed them a much bigger power: it had transformed them into the primary consumers.

Knitting was very much a part of this new economic construction. Women had been frantically knitting for half a century to cope with the harshness of life: they had used their needles to clothe their families during the Depression, and to keep soldiers warm during two World Wars; knitting was useful, patriotic; it was a nonracial craft and an ageless skill, widely practiced across the social spectrum. From teenagers to old ladies, from rich to middle-class to working-class women, everyone knew how to knit. For the yarn manufacturing companies, which had been growing steadily during World War II, the Western female population represented the biggest ever consumer market.

Postwar yarn manufacturers were quick to shift production from war items to civilian needs, targeting women as primary consumers. Knitting became an industry-driven craft. While in the past, most knitting patterns had either been passed down through generations or designed by the knitter, in the late 1940s, the knitting industry began producing patterns as marketing tools. Yarn manufacturers supplied them to publishers, who printed the patterns in books, magazines, and newspapers. These publications greatly contributed to spreading the idea that modernity meant that women should aspire to become domestic goddesses for their families; they had to learn how to clean, cook, and knit for their loved ones. Unisex patterns like the Nordic sweaters my father and I are wearing in the photograph served this purpose; they were a clever marketing tool that allowed one to knit more than one garment from the same pattern. Unisex fashion also reinforced the central role that the nuclear family had in the postwar society—parents and children wore identical homemade knitted uniforms.

As the economic boom progressed, fashion discovered knitting and crocheting, and yarn manufacturers began targeting women more and more as independent consumers and less and less as mothers and wives. In other words, patterns encouraged women to knit for themselves, to please themselves, to look fashionable and beautiful, something that had never happened before. Toward the end of the 1950s on the French and Italian Riviera, it was customary to see women knitting and crocheting in small groups under beach umbrellas, making Chanel-style suits and coats for autumn, angora sweaters for winter, and handbags to carry while shopping. It was the beginning of the realization that women were indeed powerful consumers.

Naturally, the separation of gender roles inside the nuclear family, intimately associated with peace and happiness, was a fantasy from the very beginning. In the 1950s, strong cultural undercurrents were already flowing and would eventually burst into the human rights movement, the women's liberation movement, and the antiwar movement.

For many women caught in the domestic goddess's enclave, the knitting cage became too restrictive, mostly because the relentless marketing of products to women opened a window onto the outside world, a world of infinite possibilities. Many women began feeling increasingly isolated in their marital homes, and though they sensed that there was something missing in their own lives, they were unable to understand why, or perhaps they were too afraid to confront reality. In 1963, Betty Friedan, a part-time journalist who had given up her career to get married, provided an answer to this dilemma when she published *The Feminine Mystique*, which soon became a landmark book of the American feminist movement. Friedan had interviewed her old classmates at Smith, the elite Seven Sisters women's college, and unveiled a deep sense of malaise among highly educated women. These women felt they had no choice, no avenues to channel their talents. Marriage had turned out to be an existential cage, a socioeconomic trap from which they had no idea how to get out. These women, unlike their female ancestors, were fully conscious of the walls of the yarn cage.

In the 1960s, many of my friends' mothers and my own experienced the same frustration. As Erica Jong put it, they suffered from a problem that had no name. They did not know what was wrong with their lives, why they were not satisfied by their children, their husbands, and their perfect homes.

These women carried on cooking, cleaning, and looking after

their families, but there was no joy in what they were doing; domestic work was a heavy burden and, at times, felt like a form of indentured servitude.

By the mid-1960s, many adolescent daughters looked at their mothers as role models not to follow. They trashed the image of the domestic goddess and went to war with the world to redefine womanhood. As in all major revolutions, the feminist movement had to reach ground zero to start rebuilding; everything that had been associated with female subjugation had to be wiped out.

While any type of "female" craft was widely dismissed as an instrument to reinforce the male domination paradigm, when it came to knitting and crocheting, the feminist movement was split and could not take a stand. Some women looked at knitting as a craft that had bound women to their homes and occupied them in invisible, unrewarded labor, and considered it one of the symbols of women's oppression. These women were unaware of the empowering political and revolutionary aspect that knitting has had throughout history. They also did not acknowledge the fact that it had been an effective vehicle of human creativity. Many young women, like myself, disagreed; we carried on enjoying knitting, and we were allowed to do so. We saw the needles and crochet hook as additional tools with which to fight for independence, not so much from men but from the ultimate expression of domination: capitalism. Producing your own clothes was a strong anticonsumerist statement, as exemplified by the hippie movement. Interestingly, it made it possible for knitters to live to the fullest the popular feminist slogan "I am mine." Reconquering the female body meant stripping it of pornographic male exploitation, but it also involved clothing it as one pleased, outside mainstream fashion production.

The ambivalence toward knitting and crocheting inside the feminist movement was resolved with a ploy: knitting was not political, it was personal. Women could knit during assemblies, as well as self-help and consciousness-raising weekly meetings—or they could choose not to; it was up to the individual. Knitting and crocheting were neutral activities. This is an extraordinary fact because inside the feminist movement, the primary mantra was "The personal is political." Neutrality did not exist: everything was political and nothing was personal.

How did knitting manage to become neutral? The most likely answer is that the idea that knitting was a female-oppressive craft was an untenable stereotype: Men had been knitting through the centuries, and knitters had never felt enslaved by needles and yarn. On the contrary, the ability to knit a sweater for your partner or a poncho for yourself has always been a sign of personal skill and an expression of creativity, an act of free will.

Perhaps this is why during my militant years in the Italian feminist movement, I never came across criticism about my knitting from someone who did not knit; in fact, I did teach a few close female and male friends how to knit, and watched them

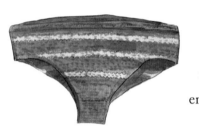

become enthusiastic knitters. Among the most popular patterns were knitted bikinis (see pattern at the end of the book). Those who did not knit and were not interested in knitting accepted the neutral status of the practice. Knitting was not celebrated, but neither was it condemned; however, many knitters used their needles and yarn as an additional instrument to promote female emancipation and liberation.

In 1975, I was a member of a feminist group in Rome that promoted the use of contraception among women. I held weekly meetings every Friday afternoon together with two female gynecologists. Part of my job was to help women choose the best contraceptive and return later on to talk about their experience. Though every week many women attended the meeting, hardly any of them ever came back, and this is why I remember the few who did, among them a mother and her teenage daughter from Sicily.

They were upper middle class, wealthy. They sat quietly, listening to the other women. During those meetings, we encouraged people to talk about their experiences, why they had decided to use their own contraceptive instead of relying upon their partner to make sure they would not get pregnant. Fully opening up to others was part of our strategy to empower these women, to teach them to take control of their bodies and their sex lives.

I generally did not knit during those meetings; I often stood in the middle of the room moderating the debate, answering questions, and booking visits with the gynecologists for the following week. But that Friday, there were not a lot of women; the meeting was running smoothly and I felt somehow comfortable with the group, so toward the end, while the gynecologists answered some questions, I sat on one of the benches and picked up my knitting, a jute beach bag I had just started.

The mother and daughter waited for everyone to leave the room before approaching me. The mother asked if we could talk in private and I was about to reply that it was not possible, our rule was that everything had to be discussed publicly, when I saw a flash of panic in the daughter's eyes. So I agreed to listen to them and we sat down next to each other on one of the benches.

They had lied to us; it was not the mother but the daughter who needed contraception. I told them that it was not a problem, but they shook their heads. She needed a consultation right away; she had just turned eighteen and she was due to get married the following week. I told them that I could not accommodate their request, there was nobody available until the following week, that was our procedure. I was about to leave them when I realized that they both were looking at me pleadingly. I sensed that they shared a terrible secret. They desperately needed help, I thought, and I was the only person who could provide it.

I told them to wait and went into the other room, where one of the gynecologists was getting ready to leave. I asked her to make an exception and do a consultation right away. She asked me what the problem was, and I told her the truth: I did not know, but I was sure there was a very good reason, and the mother and daughter were too scared to talk. She agreed to see them.

When I went back, the mother was holding my knitting in one hand and the pattern in the other. As soon as she saw me, she apologized and put them back on the bench. "Are you a knitter?" I asked. She said she was, and she added that in the commotion of leaving for the meeting, she had forgotten to bring her knitting. I picked up my knitting bag, put the pattern and my knitting inside, handed them over to her, and escorted her and her daughter into the consultation room. "You need this more than me," I told the mother. "Just bring it back with your daughter and her story."

A month later, they came back with a beautifully knit jute bag and a tragic story with a happy ending to tell the group. The daughter had been promised in marriage by her father to a distant cousin, a powerful and much older man. Her mother had been too afraid to confront her husband, so had taken the matter into her own hands. She had contacted our group and helped her daughter get contraception. If she could not stop the marriage, at least she could prevent her eighteen-year-old daughter from having a baby with a man she did not love.

Two days before the marriage, the daughter took her life into her own hands and refused to go ahead with the arranged marriage. With the help of her mother, she moved to Switzerland, where she enrolled at a boarding school to complete high school. Meeting us, getting to know our organization, had given the mother the courage and the strength to protect her daughter, and her daughter the will to take charge of her own life. The women in the room spontaneously started clapping; it was one of those magical moments of female empowerment that I will keep in my memory treasure box forever.

Knitting came fully to the forefront of feminism when it became clear that emancipation had nothing to do with women performing traditionally male roles and ditching domestic activities, when we finally admitted that by definition, equality has no gender, no race, no social status, something the hippie movement had openly professed. Interestingly, men had already begun reclaiming some of the domestic creative activities that had traditionally been performed by women, like cooking. The cooking revolution of the late 1990s and early 2000s confirmed what

Debbie Stoller, founder and editor of *Bust* magazine, summarized in her book *Stich 'n Bitch*: The feminist movement had not overturned the stereotypes of traditional society, valuing things that men do, activities done outside the home. True social change would only come when the work that women have always done was equally valued by the culture at large.

Though men knitting is not as ubiquitous as men cooking, knitting is increasingly becoming an activity that transcends gender, race, and social status. Free of any stereotype, it teaches all of us to accept the diversity of others. In a globalized world, this is yet another remarkable trait of the power of knitting.

Magali Le Huche is a well-known French author and illustrator of children's books. In 2008, she published *Hector, l'homme extraordinairement fort* (*Hector, the Extraordinarily Strong Man*). Hector works for a circus where everyone has a unique characteristic. His is that he is exceptionally strong—he can lift two washing machines with a finger. But Hector has a secret. Underneath the caravan where he lives, he has built a room where he devotes himself to his favorite activity: knitting. "One purl one stitch, from angora to mohair, from wool to cotton, knitting is my passion," he sings.

One day, the tamers of lions and leopards discover his secret, steal his knitted items, and hang them outside the circus tent to make fun of Hector. Laughing, they describe him not as the extraordinarily strong man but as the extraordinarily crazy-about-knitting man, a freak.

Hector has no time to feel sorry for himself, because an exceptionally strong wind unhinges the circus tent, which flies away with Hector's knitting, and soon everything is flying, including people's clothes. When the wind finally dies down, everybody is naked and there is nothing left to clothe them.

A naked Leopoldine, the dancer whom Hector secretly loves, finds him outside his caravan holding a beautiful tutu he has knit for her. Leopoldine puts it on, gathers all the others, and asks Hector to teach them how to knit. "One purl one stitch, from angora to mohair, from wool to cotton, knitting is our passion," they soon all sing. They knit their clothes and a new tent for the circus, which they name the Second Extraordinary Circus. The most acclaimed performance becomes Hector and Leopoldine's, a dance they do while knitting.

Smashing stereotypes is part of the long march toward progress. It is a subversive, often antiestablishment act, a revolutionary wave that women in the feminist movement caught and still continue to surf. But social change cannot be confined to one gender, cannot be limited to one race, to one social group; true social change is always universal, as universal is its rebellious push. Male, queer, and transgender knitting, especially if done in public, has been at the vanguard of modernity because it throws into question the definition of masculine and feminine. Knitting can challenge society's view of what gender looks like in everyday life, and in doing so, encourages us to be more accepting of diversity, a process through which our souls can truly shine.

In 2017, Louis Boria was photographed knitting on the New York City subway. The picture was posted by singer Frenchie Davis and immediately went viral on social media; it was inspirational for many people because it broke the traditional knitting stereotype that only women knit, and only at home. That image helped pry off one of the last bars of the yarn cage.

Boria's love affair with knitting was a revelation. His grandmother had tried to teach him to crochet when he was a teenager, but he did not like it. Years later, he had a dream that he had his hands in the air, working as if he was knitting with yarn and needles, and it had felt so good that he had decided to learn how to knit. He was immediately hooked. All he wanted to do was knit, but he was afraid to do it in public, on the subway, or on the bus. What prevented him was the stereotype of knitting as a woman's craft, and he felt uncomfortable challenging that stereotype in public; he did not want to be judged. But at the same time, he knew he was just wasting time on the subway, one hour and fifteen minutes both ways every day, going to work with his knitting in the bag. It took him some time to gather the courage to take out his knitting in public, but as soon as he began purling and stitching on the subway, people approached him, asking questions about knitting. They warmed up to him; they were kind.

Knitting on the subway changed Boria's life. Today he runs his own knitting business, Brooklyn Boy Knits, producing hand-knit clothes, and he feels complete; he is living his dream. But knitting has also been instrumental in freeing him from his fears. The yarn cage may have been mostly full of women, but others, many others, have been locked inside it.

One by one, the bars of the yarn cage are being torn out. Some have been removed by women and some by men, all of them knitters. Among these liberators are the Finnish heavy metal musicians who in July 2019 organized the first Heavy Metal Knitting World Championship. The competitors, often in constume, knit furiously onstage in time to the bands playing behind them.

There are few boundaries left. We, the knitters and the future knitters, are more and more free. What defines us is the yarn that connects us, the gift of nature we spin and knit, together, everywhere, and forever. We are breaking out of the yarn cage.

CHAPTER FIVE

Wool Is Cool

D erek is a Rastafarian house painter in his fifties from South London whom I hired to paint some rooms in my house before I rented it out. One day, he was finishing a section of the sitting room while I was knitting there and I noticed that he kept glancing over at me. I was working on a charcoal lace shawl with a very fine silk-cashmere yarn I had bought in Milan a couple of years earlier and forgotten at the bottom of an old knitting bag. I found the bag with the precious yarn and pattern while I was clearing out my storage unit. I was so happy when I saw it that I started the scarf that very evening. The pattern was complicated and I needed to be focused until I got the hang of it, but Derek's interest in my knitting kept distracting me.

"Do you knit?" I finally asked him. He shook his head but added that he used to when he was in an orphanage. He said that he loved knitting because it was the only activity that calmed his anger. I made him a cup of tea and invited him to tell me his story.

"I moved to London from Birmingham when I was eleven," he began. "My mother had got a job as a secretary and as is custom in our culture, she took me, the oldest one, with her, and left my younger brother and sister with some people she knew in Birmingham. The plan was to save enough money to have a place for all of us in London, but she fell very ill. The doctors said that she needed a kidney transplant. While we were waiting for a donor, social workers found my brother and sister living in the streets of Birmingham. They were only eight and nine years old. The people who were supposed to look after them had chucked them out suddenly. We never knew why, but I suspect that with my mother being ill, they feared she would stop sending money for them. My brother and sister were brought to London and put in a children's home.

"I remember being very angry at the time, angry at those people who had treated my brother and sister like old furniture, angry at the doctors who insisted my mother had to have a transplant, angry at the father I had never met and never even knew who he was. I was angry, angry, angry. I loved my mother, I loved her and wanted to protect her, but I was a child and I was alone.

"My mother's family, who was originally from Jamaica, had emigrated to Canada. My mother had come to the UK alone; I really do not know why. So we had no relatives here, no one to help us; we were alone."

I asked Derek if his mother taught him how to knit, and he said no but told me he used to watch her knitting just as he had been watching me a few minutes earlier. Even when people are in the middle of complex stitches, he said, there is a glow, an aura of peace around them. While you knit, the mind empties of negative thoughts and relaxes.

"Knitting is yoga for the mind," I said. He smiled, adjusted his dreadlocks inside his huge Rasta hat, nodded, and carried on with his story: "My mother died a few days after the transplant. Soon after, I was also put in the children's home. It was not a bad place, but I hated it. I was uncontrollable, I had so much anger inside that I kept running away and getting into fights. It was around that time that I became a Rastafarian; I stopped eating meat and let my hair grow. I desperately wanted a Rasta hat with the colors of the rainbow, so when they taught me how to knit, I asked to knit that hat. I got the wool and the pattern and spent hours knitting. For the first time since my mother died, I was at peace, and when the hat was finished, I was so proud of having done it myself. [See pattern at the end of the book.]

"If I think back, those were very dark years for me.

I was lost; I was alone in a world that I perceived as hostile. The few sparkling memories are knitting my hat and wearing it proudly in the children's home cafeteria and spending a weekend at the home of the woman who taught me how to knit, eating, talking, laughing, watching *Top of the Pops*, and knitting."

After he left, I reflected on what Derek had told me. I was also going through a dark period in my life. Somehow, years ago, I lost my husband; he became a different person, but I had only realized this a few weeks earlier. For years he deceived me, pretending to be himself while he gambled away our savings by investing in riskier and riskier business deals. Financial infidelity, they call it; I call it madness. I also felt at the mercy of a hostile world, but I am not angry—I am deeply, deeply sad. Luckily, writing this book has turned out to be my lifeboat in an ocean full of perils, as well as my compass directing me to a safe shore. Is this what knitting his hat had meant to Derek? Purling and stitching assisted him in navigating his anger to find peace.

One difference, for me, between writing and knitting is that knitting is not a struggle. Even when I am following a complex pattern and I keep making mistakes and having to undo my work, I never get angry, I never feel the frustration of not being able to communicate my thoughts through sentences. In general, knitters do not throw their needles in a corner and go for a run, pretending to clear their mind but in reality just trying to get rid of their frustration. They do not abandon their knitting for days to recharge; they never express doubts about their project. They plug on, because the repetitive purling and stitching is soothing, peaceful, and fun—the final product is just their bonus.

Some time ago, I came across *Knit Om*, a knitters' blog that stimulated my curiosity because of the connection between knitting and the om mantra. On the blog, I read the story of an American woman who, after she lost her father, took up knitting to keep his memory alive. She had been raised by her father and grandfather, who were both from Norway, a country famous for knitting patterns and folk stories. Both men were wonderful storytellers, so her childhood had been filled with tales of trolls and nissen, small mischievous gnomes that wear conical knitted red hats or stocking caps. Learning how to knit like a Norwegian seemed the best way to stay connected with her father and grandfather, to build a solid memory bridge between the past, the present, and the future.

She bought circular needles, a pattern for a Norwegian cowl, and the yarn, and watched a YouTube video on how to knit. She began casting on. It took a while to learn; she kept hitting rewind to rewatch the casting-on process. When she finally understood how to do it, her stitches were uneven. Some were too loose, some were too tight, but she carried on until, after a few rows, she realized that she was knitting a twisted mess. She did not know that the stitches she had placed on the circular needles had to be worked in the same direction. She was not knitting a cowl but a messy spiral. So she ripped out the work and started again.

In her post, the woman recounts how she spent days knitting, then ripping out what she had done, realizing she had made new mistakes. Yet she cast on the stitches with the same determination and commitment as she had the first time. She did not give in to frustration; on the contrary, even as she got better at casting on and then at carrying over the classic black and white yarns of the Norwegian cowl while purling and stitching, she expected to make more mistakes, and when she did, she undid the work and started all over again.

She spent days, then weeks, knitting and undoing her work. When the cheap acrylic yarn she had bought started to fall apart, she bought a better-quality yarn that would withstand the knitting-and-unraveling ritual she was performing, like Penelope waiting for Ulysses to come home. When she finally completed what she thought was a wearable circular knitted garment, she greeted it as an old friend, someone who during those weeks of grieving had held her shaky hand as she cast on, purled, stitched, and undid her work, over and over again.

I am sure Derek had to unravel his work several times before properly knitting his hat. Unlike the American Penelope, he had produced a good hat. However, what lifted the weight of his loss and hers was not the beauty and perfection of the knitted garment, it was the process of creating it.

Last night, I rummaged through my knitting bags to evaluate my stock of yarn in the hope of finding other forgotten balls of precious yarn. Because I am broke, I cannot go to one of my favorite knitting shops to buy more expensive yarn now that I have finished my shawl. Instead I go to the Oxfam thrift shop in Chelsea to see if they have some old cashmere sweaters that I can use to knit a hat. I have done this before when searching for a very fine yarn. All you need to do is properly undo the stitches at the bottom of the sweater and spool the yarn. Machine knitting is so even and has no single knots, so rolling the yarn into a big ball is quick and easy. Unfortunately, the thrift shop did not have anything I liked. So I had to revert to my stock.

At the bottom of each bag, I came across the usual messy bundles of entangled yarn. Some were as big as a small pillow and as bright as the rainbow. I took a big breath, picked up the first bundle, and began unraveling it. I must have spent more than an hour undoing it, and when I finally looked at the five balls of yarn I had freed from one another, I felt a familiar sense of achievement.

My young hairdresser recently told me that her psychologist had used exactly the same process to help her through a very tough time. The psychologist had asked her to draw a bundle of several yarns of different colors, all tangled up together. She showed me her first drawing and I smiled; it looked so familiar. How many times had I untangled multicolored balls of yarn, spending hours extracting one strand at the time, retracing the knots, gently pulling the yarn until a new knot would appear, opening the bundle at one side to loosen up the wool? How many times had I spent hours freeing one yarn at a time from a messy bundle, rolling it into a ball, and putting it back into my knitting bag?

"I was going through a tough time," my hairdresser told me. "I had broken up with my boyfriend because I knew he was not right for me—he had cheated on me; he was a narcissist—but emotionally I was still very dependent upon the relationship. I got ill; my immune system was not working properly and no one seemed to understand what was wrong with it. I also felt lost professionally. I love my job, but I hated the salon where I was working and did not have the courage to walk away. I did not earn enough to live by myself, so I rented a room in a flat with other people. They were okay, but I did not get along with them—I did not get along with anyone. I felt trapped.

"The psychologist said that the bundle of tangled yarns symbolized the different strands of my life. Basically, I was emotionally, existentially, professionally, and socially a mess. I had to identify each problem with a color: my relationship with my boyfriend was the red yarn, my work was yellow, and so on. What I needed to do was to untangle the bundle one color at the time.

"Breaking up with my boyfriend did not make me feel better; it did not solve the problem for the simple reason that our relationship was only one of the many yarns entangled in the bundle. Cutting the piece of yarn, severing the relationship, made things worse because it did not disentangle the entire bundle. On the contrary, it left part of the red yarn, part of the problem, in the middle of the bundle. If I wanted to get better, I had to pull free one yarn at a time."

While she was talking, I could hear my grandmother saying the same thing: you never cut the yarn, you work to free one strand at a time from the others. Only in very exceptional circumstances, when the knots are so, so tight and the yarns so fine that they have begun to break, can you cut, but then it's not one single yarn—you need to cut several.

Cutting the yarn is capitulating—no, it is worse than that. As my hairdresser's psychologist said, it is deserting life.

"What at the beginning looked a huge and painful task became a soothing mental routine," continued my hairdresser. "Day after day, I spent long hours untangling one problem at a time, freeing it from the others, looking at the knots, loosening them, always focused on the yarn so that it could be set free more easily. As I progressed, I drew the new shape of the bundle. When I spooled out the first yarn, I rolled it into a ball and drew it next to the bundle. Slowly I collected several rolls, each one a different color, while the bundle got smaller and looser until it was not there anymore. When I drew a line of balls, I could almost feel them in my hand. I could smell them. One by one, I put them into my knitting bag. My life was filled with order and peace again, and a way forward."

She showed me all the drawings, including the last one, in which the balls were neatly lined up inside the bag. I noticed that in all of them, she had used the same colors, but in the final one, they looked richer, even brilliant. She had gone over them several times, so that everything appeared brighter, as if the yarns had been washed clean of the dust they had accumulated while trapped inside the bundle.

My grandmother believed that the power of knitting had a 360-degree reach, from politics and economics to healing the mind and the body. Translated into more modern jargon, she was convinced that "wool is cool." Her belief was based upon personal experience, a wisdom she transmitted to me. Today, there are many scientific studies that confirm that knitting is cool, that it is good for your body and mind. It is sufficient to mention one: "Knitting and Well-Being," an academic paper based upon the results of an online survey from 3,545 knitters worldwide.

In the paper's conclusion, coauthor Betsan Corkhill, a British physiotherapist and founder of an organization called Stitchlinks that promotes knitting as a therapeutic practice, writes: "Therapeutic knitting is being used to manage the experience of pain, mental health, dementia and addiction. Therapeutic knitting groups promote purpose, creativity, success, reward and enjoyment, which is particularly important in individuals who have no experience of these in other aspects of their lives."

To summarize: Knitting helps us cope with the unexpected dark moments of our lives.

Some time ago, I visited a very dear friend in Stockholm who has cancer. One morning, I accompanied him to the hospital for his chemotherapy session. I took my knitting and a book with me. In the waiting room, there were a few people, as it was early in the morning and not many patients had arrived yet. I looked around the room, which was strangely comfortable for a hospital waiting room. It had small armchairs, a fancy espresso machine, a TV tuned to the news with the sound off and captions scrolling across the bottom of the screen, and a big glass wall with a door opening onto a courtyard. I picked up my knitting and started purling and stitching.

A couple arrived and sat down just across from me. They must have been in their late sixties, married, I thought, for a long time. The man took his coat off and went to the coffee machine. The woman took her knitting out of a big handbag. She was knitting what appeared to be a dress for a four- or five-year-old child on circular needles, using a light blue cotton yarn, so I thought it was a summer dress. I noticed that the stitches were very complicated, forming rows of raised shells with lace crests at the top. It was a beautiful pattern, and the cotton yarn made the edges of the shells look lighter, so that at a distance they resembled the foam of waves. She was not following a pattern; clearly she had memorized the sequence of the stitches and did not need any chart.

At a certain point, our eyes met and she smiled at me. I was knitting a multicolored dress for my granddaughter, but as it was November, I was using wool. My stitches were monotonous, with only a simple motif to mark the transition from the top to the waist. But the wool was very attractive and made the fabric a stripy field of rainbows.

A nurse came in and exchanged a few words with the woman before they departed together, her husband accompanying them. Her knitting was left on the armchair where she had been sitting. I waited a few minutes, but neither the woman nor her husband came back, so I stood up and got closer to read the sequence of stitches she had been knitting. As I bent over her work, someone said something in Swedish behind me. It was the woman's husband, and in response to my bemused expression, he switched to English.

He showed me the knitting pattern, which of course was in Swedish. I took a photo of it, made some notes, and thanked him. It was at that point that I noticed he had pulled his own knitting out of the woman's bag.

Peter and Ingrid, I learned, were in their late sixties and had been married for over forty years. They had four children and six grandchildren. Life had been good to them until Ingrid found out she had a nasty form of liver cancer. They had been battling it for several years. Though the cancer had gone into remission, it had come back recently, attacking other organs. Modern medicine had kept Ingrid alive well beyond their expectations, but they both doubted that she would win the fight in the end.

Ingrid had always been a knitter. When she got ill, she joined a knitting club of men and women suffering from similar illnesses who knitted for charities. Their work was handed over to refugees who arrived in Sweden with nothing. The dress she was knitting was for a little Syrian girl who was going to be a flower girl at her big sister's wedding.

Peter began knitting when Ingrid's cancer returned after her first remission. He needed something to relax, to escape from the nightmare of losing her. Her second illness had also triggered anxiety in him, which in turn produced high blood pressure, high cholesterol, and heart palpitations. Ingrid suggested knitting might improve his health, and she was right. The purling and stitching helped calm him down, curb his anxiety, lower his blood pressure and cholesterol, and even rid him of the palpitations. Of course he was on medication for his conditions as well, but since he had become a knitter, his doctors had considerably reduced the doses.

Peter did not knit for charities—he knit for politics. When he told me that, I looked at him with sincere fascination. Was he a yarn bomber? I asked. He laughed; no, he was not. He was too old to go around the city knitting graffiti on monuments. He was a political knitter. He knit squares and buttons for protests. He showed me his collection, and I found it quite impressive. Buttons to bring awareness about Facebook, Amazon, and the role of Parliament in politics; squares to denounce anti-immigration policies; I particularly liked an evil-eye glove meant to remind us that "we, the people" are watching what politicians are doing.

What did Peter do with all these items? He left them in public places, at the library, in the seats at movie theaters, on the shelves of the supermarket, anywhere someone might pick them up, look at them, and think about what they meant.

He *was* a yarn bomber, I thought, but he did not know it, or he was too modest to admit it. What really mattered to him was to feel socially and politically connected, to reach out to the world while he was in the long, dark tunnel of Ingrid's illness. Knitting was doubly beneficial to him: it improved his physical health *and* his mental health.

When I got home to my friend's house, I looked up knitting politics.wordpress. com, a web page Peter had mentioned. I could not understand who they were. The site said, "Come for the knitting and stay for the politics." Pictures of knitted squares and buttons were followed by political statements and declarations, and at the bottom of the page, it offered patterns of the knitted items for people to use. Their Twitter account had just 360 followers! But they do exist, and Peter had found them. That was all that really mattered to him.

WE ARE ALL LINKED THROUGH A GLOBAL YARN THAT KEEPS US CONNECTED

Listening to the story of Peter and Ingrid, I once again felt the wisdom of my grandmother blowing over me. Because we knit, we are all linked through a global yarn that keeps us connected, a long, tangible strand of tiny segments of materials produced by nature and spun by us. What connects us is not a Facebook page, not a Twitter account in a freezing-cold cyberuniverse, but the fruits of our earth: wool, silk, and cotton, and how we use them for the needs of the body and the mind. From the cotton fields of Egypt to the wool of the sheep of Sweden to the hair of the yaks of Mongolia, the yarn we knit reminds us that we all belong to this planet, we are all part of the miracle of life.

The mantra we recite one stitch at a time is the om of life: *We are not alone*—we share pain, sorrow, and despair as well as hope, joy, and happiness.

CHAPTER SIX

The Magic *of* *the* Knitting Networks

Pioneer women were knitters. Some were better than others, but overall, knitting was a necessary skill on the trail west, a hard march toward a constantly moving frontier. Before embarking on the journey west, women knitted socks, long johns, sweaters, hats, scarfs, blankets, everything the family would need during the long and perilous journey. The women knew that they were leaving civilization behind and had to bring with them all the items necessary to reach their destination. Knitting needles and yarn were once again part of the survival kit.

On the trail west, women kept knitting to supply the clothing they and their families needed. They knit on the wagons during the day and in the evenings by the campfire; after cooking and cleaning, they sat around the fire, forming a knitting circle. Pioneer women always carried their needles and yarn in the pockets of their aprons. Knitting was like breathing, a necessity and a habit at the same time.

It was also common for pioneer women to barter knitted garments on the trail west. Socks were always in high demand, especially among men who had nobody to knit for them: farmers in search of new land, or miners who traveled west alone to find their fortune. Around 1850, in Oregon's Willamette Valley, socks became a sort of legal tender. Women would sell a pair of socks for 50 cents' worth of groceries. The grocer then resold the socks for 75 cents a pair to the storekeeper at the mines, who in turn asked for twice that amount from his customers. Like beaver pelts and wheat, knitted socks were as good as hard currency.

In a Puritan society where women could not work, trade, or be engaged in politics, let alone vote, knitting for profit became a valued way into mainstream economics. In the settlements and cities out west, less well-off women were allowed to sell their knitting. Lower-class women sold their knitting on consignment or bartered it for goods and services. They made knitted garments for wealthy ladies and advertised their services as washerwomen. While wool stockings were easy to wash, silk stockings were very difficult: the colors would run, and water could ruin the fabric, so they were not very frequently washed.

Like a prayer, the clicking sound of the knitting needles brought comfort and hope to women thrown into an unknown world full of peril, violence, and harshness. And it eased their solitude. Mary Carpenter was a young pioneer widow who lived in a very isolated spot, far away from any neighbor. Fearful of being attacked in the night, she would hide her children in the vegetable cellar beneath the cabin and spent each night knitting in the dark, her chair positioned on the planks over the entrance to the cellar. During the blizzard of 1888 in Oxford, Nebraska, at the height of the storm, pioneer women passed the night knitting by candlelight to remain calm.

Women who survived the trail and settled in the new land often gathered together to knit whatever was needed to turn their cabins into homes. They walked long distances to a neighbor's house for the pleasure of knitting together, re-creating indoors the fireside knitting circles of the trail. During these meetings, the women unraveled the yarn of the memories they had carried with them all the way across an ocean and then a continent, and knitted to reproduce the accessories of the life they had left behind, items of a home they would never see again. They exchanged patterns and stitches from their home countries—lace from Germany, Aran from Ireland—and adapted them to their spare environment, creating new items to meet the needs of frontier life. Knitting blankets, tablecloths, and curtains provided them with a sense of normalcy in a raw land. And as the women bonded through knitting, their families slowly emerged from the isolation of carving a new existence through extreme violence and unbearable suffering. Communities were born; shops, schools, and churches were built; a railway line was laid down where caravans had marked the trail west. Eventually, lawlessness receded and faraway territories became states. Progress and modernity came to the North American continent, or at least to most of it.

Across the Continental Divide, on Vancouver Island in British Columbia, Salish women of the Cowichan tribe joined such circles at the beginning of the last century; European women and missionaries who came to their land taught them how to knit. Originally weavers who wove blankets out of yarn spun from mountain goats and a breed of now extinct small dog, the Cowichan women have mastered the craft of knitting and designed patterns with symbols of their culture and their land, knitting into the patterns the stories of their lives. Cowichan sweaters and cardigans replaced the traditional winter coats made from buffalo hide or deerskin hand-painted with symbols and drawings recounting tribal tales. Knitting has become a way for Salish women to gain financial independence, which explains why they have passed on this beautiful art to their daughters and granddaughters.

The hand-spun yarn that these Native American tribes use is the yarn of freedom, independence, and true life. Across an ocean and a continent, it links the young girls learning how to knit under the supervision of their grandmothers to myself, a little girl in Rome knitting and listening to my own grandmother's magical stories. My grandmother and I may not have inserted the story of our family into our patterns as these women do, but in my memory, each knitted item we produced together is a paragraph or a chapter of the story of who we are, where we come from, and where we are going.

The mystique of knitting, its power, is still guiding me through my present difficulties, as I imagine it is guiding women and men from all walks of life across the world. We knitters are united, forever stitched together between purl and knit, individuals interlinked by the beauty of this craft. Connected by natural fibers spun together, we are a testimony to the best attributes of humanity.

Some time ago, I came across a moving knitting story written by Kim Harris, a woman from Toronto. She wanted to knit a pair of socks using the Kitchener stitch, but she was struggling to get the technique right using online tutorials and videos, so she decided to go to the Knitting Collective in downtown Toronto, a monthly meeting at which people exchange knitting ideas and techniques, to find someone who could show her the stitch. She arrived late, when the auditorium was already full, and she was surprised to see how many people were attending the meeting.

As she found a seat, a woman with a microphone was calling out a category: cardigans and lace. Several people stood up to show their work in the category, so that whoever was knitting something similar and needed advice could approach them. The next category called was baby clothes. A woman stood up with what Harris described as "a sweater the size of a Christmas ornament," far, far too small to fit even a newborn. It was for a premature baby.

Baby clothes are not widely sold in premature-baby sizes, and this is a big problem for parents. "We could not put our daughter in the newborn clothes we had bought. She was too tiny—she weighed just two kilos," explained the daughter of a good friend of mine who had a premature baby girl in a London hospital. "We did find a couple of websites that sold some very expensive preemie clothes, and we bought a couple of items." Luckily, the hospital provided the baby with tiny hats, blankets, and clothes that fit her, all hand-knit, probably by knitters like the woman in Toronto. "The nurses dressed the baby every day; we could not do that because she was too delicate," continued my friend's daughter. "I remember that it was so special seeing her wearing those clothes. Because we could not get anything that fit her, seeing little knitted hats on her tiny head made a big difference to us. Wearing those clothes made her look like a person, and seeing her every day in a new outfit definitely lifted our spirits."

The outfit that the woman in Toronto was showing had been

knit for a different premature baby, one, she said, who "was not going home." A respectful silence fell over the auditorium. Her knitting group was aware that their preemie outfits would be worn by some tiny babies who were not going to survive. They knit the clothes not only so that parents could put something nice on their babies as they waited for them to grow to fit into newborn-size clothes, but also for those parents whose babies would be buried. I cannot fully imagine the pain of those mothers and fathers who are handed their child's first and last outfit, but I can appreciate that hand-knit clothes may bring them a little bit of comfort.

Those outfits the size of Christmas ornaments are proof that someone else cares. We may all be helpless, but it does matter that each stitch has been cast on and knit with love, not necessarily by a relative or a friend, but by an anonymous knitter, someone with true compassion for the joys and tragedies of others.

Knitters are often altruistic and knit less for themselves than for others: for family members, friends, charities, and various causes. Knitting groups and networks, the modern version of the pioneer women's knitting circles, are major promoters of knitting for a cause.

In 2017, Jayna Zweiman, cofounder of the Pussyhat Project, which created the hand-knit pink hats that people wore at the Women's March on Washington on January 21, 2017, launched another project, Welcome Blanket.

Using two thousand miles of yarn, approximately the length of the wall that Donald Trump wants to build between the United States and Mexico, knitters were encouraged to knit blankets for immigrants, to welcome and cuddle them. The message of the project is clear: immigrants should be embraced, not shut out. Because each blanket comes with a personal note from the maker, detailing their own immigration history, as well as advice for living in the United States, the initiative connects the new immigrants to the pioneers through these modern knitters, a purl between two stitches.

Across the United States, knitting groups have joined the challenge and carried on knitting. When pictures of immigrant children who had been separated from their parents and locked in outdoor cages near the border began surfacing, people were horrified. The children looked terrified and cold, lying on the dirt, tightly holding the Mylar blankets they had been given. Women involved in the Welcome Blanket project took their needles and yarn and began knitting soft, warm blankets for them.

As usual, grandmothers are at the forefront of the knitting world. Their wisdom is ever so strong, as is their courage. Since 2012, the Australian group Knitting Nannas Against Gas have been waging a fierce war against the mining and gas industry all over the country, using their yarn, needles, and patterns as powerful tools for change. What started as a local protest in Lismore, New South Wales, became a national movement.

Clare Twomey and Lindy Scott founded the group out of frustration; they got tired of discussing what to do at meetings and decided to take action. They went to Metgasco, a petroleum and exploration company operating in Lismore, to check out what the company was doing on their land. On their first outing, they brought chairs and tea, but they wanted to take action, so they decided to bring their needles and yarn the next time and spend the time knitting. Sound familiar? It is indeed what the tricoteuses did in front of the guillotine. The nannas mostly knit in yellow and black, the colors of the Lock the Gate Alliance, a group formed to raise awareness about the dangers of coal and gas mining. And of course they knit protest items: hats, scarves, blankets.

Since their first meeting in Lismore, new groups of Knitting Nannas have been formed across Australia; women gather together, and while they knit and drink tea, they watch what is going on, including how the coal companies and the politicians collude. Because the nannas are of a certain age, they carry an aura of wisdom, and might appear fragile, although they are not. They have turned their age and wisdom into a powerful weapon to defend our planet.

My grandmother would not have become a Knitting Nanna; she had been brought up to remain in the shadows, and the idea of stepping into the limelight would have been an uncomfortable one for her. But in private, while knitting with me, she would be cheering the nannas for challenging an industry that devalues people and the environment in the name of profits. I think she would be shocked at the level of pollution brought about by "progress and modernity," and she would be deeply concerned about climate change. My grandmother lived in harmony with the seasons, which marked the rhythm of her existence. It was a magical cycle she embraced each year in her daily activities, including gardening, shopping, cooking, and of course knitting, during which she would regale me with stories of spring in Rome, when the smell of blossoms made everyone happy, or the cold wind of January, which brought to the city the scent of snow from the surrounding hills.

Our knitting, like the fruits and vegetables we bought at the open-air food market down the street, was seasonal. In July and August, we ate delicious tomato and onion salads and knit with cotton; in the fall, my grandmother cooked apples with cinnamon, and we knit using mixed wool and cotton yarns; and in winter, we feasted on carrots, potatoes, and beets, and we knit in wool, always in tune with the weather, which was perfectly predictable. There was nothing monotonous in the certainty of the seasons and the weather; on the contrary, by the time one season was waning, we were ready for the change, eager to knit new patterns with different yarn, to eat new foods and wear different clothes. Even the thunderstorms that inevitably arrived in mid-August were welcome, as they ended long summers and cooled the air, washing away the dust and making Rome as brilliant as the jewel it was.

I miss that beauty, the security of a life in tune with the rule of nature, a predictable seasonal nature. Somewhere during my existence, that rhythm got out of sync; it slowly faded away, blurred in the pollution and mechanics of a high-tech existence. I want it back, but I do not know how to get it.

While researching this book I came across WARM, an environmental knitting project in Victoria, Australia, created by a group of artists and knitters who joined together to knit a huge mural. The inspiration came from a sheep farmer, a modern shepherd who was not able to keep his herd due to climate change. Knitters were asked to knit ponds, flowers, grass, trees, birds, and windmills to be stitched together over a gigantic image of a destroyed land. "If we cannot bring back nature, let's knit it back"— the WARM knitters made a powerful statement to bear witness that the killing of nature is not just "another" genocide, it is the genocide of all humanity.

During the Australian summer of 2019–2020, about a billion animals were killed in the wildfires that burned across the country. Knitters from all over the world got their needles and yarn and began producing mittens, socks, and little ponchos to protect the animals from the heat. We need each other. As creatures of the same planet, we are dependent upon each other. And without animals, our world could not exist.

A dear friend of mine who is a Franciscan monk recently told me a story about the similarities between sheep and us. We were talking about the parable of the missing sheep. Why does Jesus, the shepherd, go search for the missing sheep? Here is what he told me. A herd of sheep was crossing a big road, a sort of motorway with a metal guardrail in the middle. One ewe got separated from the herd, and in her panic, she went crazy, hitting her head against the guardrail, trying to commit suicide. The herding dogs ran back to look for her, finding her with blood streaming from her head. Just like that sheep, a man separated from other people goes crazy, loses the will to live; his existence ceases to make any sense.

Have we all lost our minds in a world ruled by individualism and greed? Are we committing suicide like the sheep separated from the others in the middle of the motorway? Are we ending our existence without knowing it by simply destroying this beautiful planet? Are we so blinded by our own narcissism that only children and teenagers can see what we are doing? I think that perhaps I should approach those kids who are demonstrating against climate change every Friday, the followers of Greta Thunberg, who beg us to stop this insanity, to end the construction of the global Babylon. I should teach them how to knit their protest, as the artists of WARM did and as my grandmother would probably have done. The question is: Do we have enough time to knit a way to save the planet?

CHAPTER SEVEN

Knitting *in the* Age *of* Neuroscience

I am spending my first spring in the Rockies, and even if it is still cold, nature is exploding under the lukewarm rays of a constantly clouded but magnificent sky, lifting clouds of pollen everywhere. I am seriously on edge. Until now, I have managed to navigate the high-stress waves of the last months without getting sick. This has been a blessing because I have been able to channel all my energies into developing strategies to clear up the financial mess my husband has created. I am not out of the woods yet, far from it. I have not sold the lake house where I am currently staying, so I still need to pay the huge monthly expenses associated with it, and I cannot afford to do that for much longer. I must develop another financial scheme, I must act quickly, and to do that, I need to keep my head clear, literally and figuratively.

The stress that comes with battling to avoid financial ruin is catching up with me. A few days ago, I lost my cool. It happened suddenly, during a surge of hay fever. I hung up the phone with the bank manager and burst into tears. I could not stop crying. I cried for my long-gone marriage, for the home I love and will soon no longer have, for the humiliation of financial distress, and for my own stupidity in believing that a man, any man, could handle the responsibility of my life. I cried in the garden while raking the winter leaves and picking up broken branches; I cried in the garage while sweeping the dust that had accumulated under the winter snow; I sobbed in the house, room by room, searching for boxes of Kleenex. I cried because down the road they were cutting huge trees to build yet another McMansion; I cried for this beautiful little village now turned into a playground for the super-rich, for the water of the lake polluted by the oil spills of the trains that relentlessly carry the products of fracking from eastern Montana and North Dakota to the Pacific. I even cried because of global warming, the indifference of our race to the destruction of our planet.

The more I cried, the less I could breathe. My chest was so tight, as if a huge rock had been placed inside my rib cage. Then, suddenly, my heart started its old trick. It was beating in my throat, faster and faster and faster. I have been on medication for a while for a condition called curling, in which the top half of the heart turns to one side and the bottom goes the opposite way. It is a serious condition because this movement damages the valve, building a prolapse inside it and reducing its efficiency. I became dizzy and decided to lie down on the couch, tears streaming out of my eyes, unable to move, listening to the uncontrollable beating of my heart.

Maria, my Latina housekeeper, found me there, with my hands on my chest, battling a panic attack. After twenty-six years, Maria is a dear friend. She loves me and I love her. When I am alone in this isolated house in the middle of the woods, facing the lake, she stays with me. She is a remarkable woman who has had a very tough life. Born wealthy but caged inside a macho family, she found her independence and freedom in the US as a waitress and cleaner, far from her home. She raised three kids on her own, cleaning houses and working in restaurants across the country. She is intelligent and kind, and she is a super knitter. Through the years, we have spent long hours knitting and talking, telling each other secrets, sharing problems, and giving each other advice. She knows me well, and this is why she did not call an ambulance, did not take me to the hospital. She sat next to me and gently stroked my head, reminding me how far down the road of financial recovery I had already come.

When I finally stopped crying, she made lemon-ginger tea with honey for both of us and helped me sit down to drink it. While I sipped the tea, we started talking. After a while, she took out her knitting and began working the sleeves of an Aran sweater for her son's girlfriend. At a certain point, she asked me to try on the sleeves to see if they were too tight. As I slipped the wool over my hand and wrist, I felt the warmth of the fabric, the comfort of its embrace. I stroked the complicated pattern and told her that it was beautiful, so nicely knitted. She smiled and offered me my knitting, a scarf with a simple lace pattern I had designed. "Loretta," she said, stroking the knitted fabric, "look how soft this is." She remembered that I'd brought that merino wool back from New Zealand a few years earlier. I held the fabric in my palm gently, as if it were a precious object. I thought, *When winter comes, this scarf will warm my neck with its gentle embrace, a loving, long-lasting hug. When winter comes, I will be out of this mess, I just need to get through the next few months.*

All I wanted to do in that moment was purl and knit that amazing yarn into a comfort blanket to shelter me from the tempest of my dark feelings. I picked up my needles and began knitting. We sat together, knitting and talking, for a long time, as the sun went down on the back of the mountains, until the reflection of the light disappeared from the empty lake and darkness arrived. I do not know when my heart stopped curling, when its beating left my throat and moved back down into my rib cage, when the tears stopped rolling down my cheeks and I could clearly see the stitches I was knitting. But when it was time to go to bed, I was back in control, I was healed, I was myself.

Neuroscience tells us that when we are in a stressful situation, our brain sends stress hormones through nerve pathways. Our reactions depend on the amount of stress hormones our brains produce and on how we deal with this chemical phenomenon. Although during the previous months, while facing much more challenging situations, I had kept my cool, that day I was overwhelmed by the stress; I could not counteract it, and I ended up suffering a panic attack.

Performing something repetitive and rhythmic such as yoga or breathing into a small paper bag or knitting induces relaxation, which we now know neutralizes the stress hormones. Relaxation is the antithesis of stress: it lowers blood pressure, raises energy levels, improves the body's management of blood sugar, and even slows down the process of aging. However, like yoga, knitting is much more than a relaxing activity.

Scientists tell us that because knitting is a two-handed, cross-body coordinated movement, it requires the two sides of the brain to communicate with each other and share information effectively. Tai chi is an example of a two-handed, cross-body coordinated exercise. Children who have problems with spatial perception are advised to practice tai chi to improve the joint functioning of the left brain and the right brain. Knitting is also rhythmic, repetitive, and automatic; plus, all these actions are performed at once. Even if purling and stitching seems easy— and indeed, it quickly becomes second nature for knitters— processing all these movements simultaneously takes a lot of brain capacity, and the more brain capacity we apply to knitting, or any other activity, the less there is available to worry.

Neuroscientists have isolated the areas stimulated in the brain by knitting, areas that correspond to tasks such as paying attention and planning (the frontal lobe), processing sensory and visual information (the parietal lobe), storing memory (the occipital lobe), and coordinating the precision and timing of movements (the cerebellum). Accessing all these areas stimulates the connection between nerve cells (neurons) and keeps their interactions smooth and efficient. Neurons are electrically excitable cells of the brain, spinal cord, and peripheral nerves. The billions of neurons in our body receive signals from every sense, control movement, create memories, and form the neural basis of every thought. As we age, the more we use these connections, the more we stimulate the neurons, the more we keep our brain fit, mitigating illnesses such as dementia.

Knitting is more than relaxing; it is a workout for the brain (see pattern at the end of the book).

In 2014, a group of knitters in Australia decided to demonstrate the benefits of knitting on the brain through Neural Knitworks, a traveling exhibition that became part of National Science Week at the Hazelhurst Regional Gallery and Arts Centre in Gymea, a suburb of Sydney.

The Neural Knitworks initiative is based on the principle that yarn craft, with its mental challenges, social connection, and mindfulness, helps keep our minds sharp, engaged, and healthy. Knitters were invited to knit hundreds of neurons, which were assembled into a gigantic installation.

I did not participate in Neural Knitworks, but on the evening I experienced a panic attack, I was healed by the neurological power of knitting. Knitting brought me back to my reality, to the status of mindfulness. It lifted my mind out of the nightmare of negative scenarios, a dark hypothetical future. It also blocked in my subconscious painful memories of events that took place in my childhood, images that always reactivate old traumas, situations badly handled because of my parents' immaturity and my young age. It is unquestionable that over the past few months, knitting through my current difficulties had grounded me in the positive aspects of my present. The knitted fabric symbolizes my troubled past growing further away, row after row, and the yarn represents my bright future, today neatly stored in a merino ball.

Because I have been so focused on solving my financial problems, I find it hard to relax. I fear that if I switch off, even for an hour, I will never be able to get back into focus. I find it difficult to read a book and impossible to exercise, for the first time ever in my life. I am constantly afraid of losing my concentration. Knitting is my dear companion; it has become my emotional, intellectual, and physical safety net, as well as my primary source of dopamine, the hormone that makes us feel happy.

In need of a challenge to occupy my mind away from my anxiety, I rummaged through the leftover yarn I keep in my knitting bag at the lake house. I selected a few bright yarns and began knitting a Klein bottle. A Klein bottle is essentially an absurd object springing from a mathematical formula. It is shaped like an ampoule, a bottle with a long bent neck that curves around and enters one side, so that the opening of the neck is, improbably, inside the bottle. I came across it while researching the connection between knitting and mathematics, and I was stunned by the beauty of both the glass version and the knitted replica. I was also intrigued by the geometrical drawings of the Klein bottle on my computer screen: essentially, it is made from a single thin sheet that bends around and enters itself, intersecting without breaking in two.

I am not a mathematician or a scientist, but after reading hundreds of blogs by scientists who knit and watching their videos to see how they use knitting to visualize formulas and concepts, I understood that there is much more to knitting than we know. Natural phenomena such as birds' nests and seashells are built using the same construction method as knitting: essentially, they are structures created one line at the time, interlinked with each other horizontally and vertically, a methodology that provides stability and strength that scientists call additive manufacturing. Because of this construction, knitting can be used to produce physical models of any surface or shape, as proven by Professor Sarah-Marie Belcastro of Smith College, whose knitted Klein bottle I copied in order to de-stress.

Knitting helps us understand mathematical objects, writes Professor Belcastro: "A knitted object is flexible and can be physically manipulated, unlike beautiful and mathematically perfect computer graphics. And the process itself offers insights: in creating an object anew, not following someone else's pattern, there is deep understanding to be gained. To craft a physical instantiation of an abstraction, one must understand the abstraction's structure well enough to decide which properties to highlight. Such decisions are a crucial part of the design process, but for the specifics to make sense, we must first consider knitting geometrically."

Knitting is so versatile that it can be used to produce models of the most complex objects, such as a hyperbolic plane. Hyperbolic planes are spaces of negative curvatures (think of the shape of a horse saddle) where all lines curve away from each other, which means they are parallel only at one point and then diverge from each other. They are the opposite of a spherical plane, where all lines curve toward each other, as on the surface of a ball. Good examples of hyperbolic planes are the frills on a sea slug, the growth patterns of coral, or the way the brain folds.

Building precise physical models of hyperbolic objects with paper or plastic is impossible because of the rigidity of these materials, but using yarn and knitting needles or a crochet hook is a different story.

In 1997, Professor Daina Taimina of Cornell University crocheted the first model of a hyperbolic plane in order to visualize and prove the validity of the revolutionary mathematical formula of hyperbolic geometry: two straight lines that do not intersect each other are not necessarily parallel. You knit a hyperbolic plane by increasing the number of stitches in each row. Professor Taimina calculated the correct ratio with which to increase the stitches and produced a perfect replica of the wavy frills on the back of a sea slug. She then traced two straight lines across the fabric, which did not intersect. According to Euclidean geometry, these lines should be parallel. But when she folded her crocheted hyperbolic plane, as you can see in the video of her TED Talk, it became clear that the two lines were parallel only in the middle of the fabric, then diverged from each other toward each end and would never intersect. Professor Taimina's crochet sample proved that the principle of hyperbolic geometry that replaces the Euclidean postulate of the parallel lines is correct.

Why do we care about hyperbolic geometry? Because it helps us understand nature and the shape of our universe. Knitting contributes to unveiling the big picture of who and where we are, bringing more clarity to the laws of physics. Physicist Elisabetta

Matsumoto, a knitter since childhood, described knitted fabrics as a type of metamaterial, essentially engineered materials that get their properties not from their base material—i.e., the yarn—but from their designed structure. Depending on the sequence of stitches and patterns, knitted fabrics have very different properties from the yarn we use to produce them. Amazingly, while the yarn is not elastic, all knitted materials are stretchy. Knitting has given the yarn additional characteristics.

Matsumoto is convinced that there is a massive wealth of knowledge in the knitting community that, if translated into a quantitative model, could be beneficial in developing new products for industrial sectors, including the aerospace industry. I would add that such knowledge comes from millennia of experimentation, results that have been passed on through generations, not only through lessons on how to knit but also through storytelling. Knitters are great custodians of oral history; while they knit, they tell each other stories about life, as my grandmother did with me. Often those stories refer directly to knitting, such as how a variation on a stitch pattern produced something new or how to hide a love note in the cable stitches of a pair of socks made for a fiancé. The true power of knitting cannot be found in books, magazines, or web pages rich in patterns—sometimes it is encoded in the real-life stories passed on from one generation to the next and stored in the knitter's memory and experience. As a knitter, Professor Matsumoto knows this, and she has acquired her ancestors' wisdom, but to truly tap into the universal wealth of knowledge of knitting, she must gain access to the oral heritage of all knitters.

Unlocking what she describes as "the knitting code," the mathematical formulas behind the combinations of stitches that produce knitted fabrics' various properties, is a monumental task. If she succeeds, knitting could help us create new materials for various uses: for example, stretchable replacements for torn ligaments.

So far, a team of French physicists has developed a rudimentary mathematical model to describe the elasticity of a knitted fabric. The inspiration came when one of the physicists, Frederic Lechenault, watched his pregnant wife knitting baby booties and blankets and realized that after they were stretched, they reverted to their original shape; in other words, pulling and bending the fabric creates energy. The team has isolated three main factors: the bendiness and the length of the yarn, and the number of crossing points in each stitch. The elasticity comes from how the loops that connect the row below to the one above are knit.

Any knitter instinctively knows these principles and will choose a rib stitch for the sleeves and border of a baby sweater, to make sure that the fabric will easily stretch when put on the child and then revert to its original size to stay nicely fitted around the baby's wrists. This knowledge comes from sharing, from interacting with each other, generation after generation. Today, books and videos can help, but as Kim Harris, the woman in Toronto who wanted to knit a pair of socks using the Kitchener stitch, wrote, when you are stuck, you need to work together with a knitter.

Knitting is a constant experimentation with the yarn, no matter how simple the pattern is, and because of this, knitting challenges and stimulates the brain. Though scientists have proven the benefits of knitting, from lowering blood pressure to releasing dopamine, I believe there is a much deeper, ancient connection between the way our brains function and crave problem-solving and the craft of knitting.

Anthropologists have proven that one of the first activities of our Paleolithic ancestors was tracking animals' movements. They learned how to follow the animals by recognizing the tracks they made on the land; this has been a fundamental skill for hunting prey, whose meat provided animal fat to feed our large brains. Louis Liebenberg, a researcher at Harvard University, even believes that tracking was a critical step in our evolution. He makes the case that the art of tracking involves the same intellectual and creative abilities as physics and mathematics, and may very well represent the origin of science itself.

Tracking is an integral part of knitting. A good knitter is always able to find where he is on the map of a pattern by retracing the stitches and rows he has produced. Today there are markers, charts, and even apps that record what we are knitting, but in the past, knitters had to keep count of the rows and the stitches in their heads, and had to memorize the patterns. Being able to retrace our work, to leave our own tracks on the knitted fabric, is fundamental to avoiding mistakes. A good knitter is always able to place her next stitch in its exact location in the pattern chart.

Following a knitting pattern is similar to traveling through an unknown area using a topographic map. The journey is guided by symbols and signs that constitute a code, a specific language. Rivers, hills, mountains, and roads are marked on paper along the route, and they represent a living space, a little corner of our world. Knitting patterns are constructed in the same way: they mark on paper different stitches that reproduce a living fabric. But while the topographic map offers us the opportunity to experience an already existing environment, knitting patterns allow us to produce one of our own.

Today, we do not need to use navigation skills; the GPS on our smartphones replaces the mental effort of storing and remembering the spaces through which we have traveled or the visual image of the map we have just consulted. As our spatial cognitive capacities are becoming obsolete, they suffer from atrophy. Knitting maintains such functions because it stimulates the hippocampus, also known as the map reader of the brain, as proven by a study conducted in 2011 by Dr. Yonas E. Geda, a psychiatrist at the Mayo Clinic in Rochester, Minnesota. The results showed that among people aged seventy to eighty-nine, knitters and crocheters had the healthiest brains and memories.

Neuroscience tell us that reading maps and developing navigational skills can cause the hippocampus and the brain to grow, forming more neural pathways as the number of mental maps increases. A University College London study tested the brains of London black-cab drivers with MRIs and found that their brains grew and adapted to help them store detailed mental maps of the city. Black-cab drivers do not use GPS—to get a license, they have to prove that they have memorized the locations of all the streets of Greater London, a very demanding learning process known as the Knowledge.

Though a similar scientific study to test the growth of the knitter's brain has not been conducted, it is likely that reading and following knitting patterns, as well as knitting itself, has a similar effect on the brain. The researchers who participated in Dr. Geda's study at the Mayo Clinic seem to agree with this conclusion. They have speculated that knitting promotes the development of neural pathways in the brain that help us to maintain cognitive health.

I am not a scientist and I am not a good knitter. I am a woman struggling to make sense of a situation I never imagined I could be in. Over the past few months, I have experienced all the symptoms of stress, despair, and at times even depression. I have been lost many times in the nightmare of the future, I have doubted I would ever see the light at the end of the tunnel. Throughout this ordeal, knitting has helped me keep my sanity, anchoring me to life, making me strong, enhancing the power of my mind, making me a better writer and perhaps even a better person. As my silent companion, encouraging me to purl and stitch through adversity, knitting has also been my comfort zone, a place to which I could retreat in the long, dark nights of winter. And as spring comes and I begin knitting cotton patterns in a house I will soon leave, a house I love and thought would be mine forever, knitting has helped me to accept this big change.

I feel ready for the next chapter of my life, wherever it will take me, because I know that wherever I go, I will not be alone. I will carry with me the craft my grandmother handed me, the gift of knowledge that scientists are trying to unveil, a true treasure. And this is all I need.

CHAPTER EIGHT

Let's Knit Together: Restitching Society

When I lived in San Francisco, my first husband often went to Alaska for work and would come back with amazing stories about life in freezing-cold, remote places. I have always been fascinated with cold climates and drawn to icy landscapes. Twenty years later, I finally made it to Alaska and was mesmerized by its natural beauty and its history. And in my travels, I learned directly from Alaskan Natives about their connection to knitting.

Alaska is the last pioneer frontier of the North American continent, reached by the first Russian and European traders and explorers in the mid-1800s. To the Russians and Europeans, Alaska's indigenous population appeared to be backward, uncivilized people living in appalling conditions. Men and women were segregated from one another in underground houses framed with driftwood or whale bones, covered with sod, and connected through subterranean tunnels. Women resided in small, single-family dwellings with their daughters and sons. At age five, boys were moved to the big central structure where the men lived, socialized, relaxed, worked, and conducted politics.

Women could enter the men's quarters only to bring food during festivities, and men were allowed to visit women's dwellings at night, but had to be gone by dawn. The men hunted and fished, and the women cleaned and prepared the meat for eating. The women did not spin the fur or hair of the animals into yarn, nor did they knit; however, they produced very comfortable outfits with furs and leather using amazing needlework techniques.

For thousands of years, Alaskan Natives lived off the plants and animals of a very hostile land, thanks to the communal structure of a basic sustenance economy. Their strong tribal identity made them embrace the principle of sharing, which guaranteed their survival and, at the same, made them respect the segregation of the sexes.

The civilization that Russian and European traders and explorers brought to Alaska could not coexist with the Alaskan Natives' way of life. The destruction of the tribal system came at the hands of missionaries, who converted the Alaskan Natives to Christianity and ended the segregation between men and women, which the missionaries regarded as promiscuous because the Alaskan Natives were not monogamous. Women were no longer autonomous in their dwellings; they had to share their quarters with men. Soon, the principle of sharing clashed with the concept of ownership encoded in the colonizers' culture and economy. Men were encouraged to stop hunting for the tribe as a whole and hunt just for their own families. Marx would say that their workforce stopped belonging to the community and became their own individual property, to dispose of as they pleased. The same can be said for the women: they ceased to work for the tribe and each worked for her own family. The formation of new family units deeply altered the socioeconomic equilibrium of the Alaskan Natives, weakening their communal spirit and their group identity.

Colonizers also brought with them a cash-based capitalist economy unknown to the Alaskan Natives and out of sync with their economic tribalism. Money became a means of exchange to buy goods, including new, foreign, imported products such as flour, which belonged to the colonizers' diet. Inevitably, goods that added comfort to life in the Arctic Circle entered the Alaskan Natives' diet. But they had to find the cash to buy these goods, which was not easy for people who had always worked as members of a tribal community. As the traditional sustenance economy faded away, those who could not adapt to these radical changes fell into poverty.

The original Alaskan Native society had been much more egalitarian than Western society. Wealth was often redistributed at annual feasts and ceremonies, and families took care of one another; nobody went hungry or homeless inside the tribe. As the communal economy disintegrated and people had to individually earn a living to survive, Alaskan Natives struggled to continue living off the land as their ancestors had done. Hunting, fishing, and gathering food were not sufficient to generate the cash to stay afloat in the colonizers' economy. Families needed other income.

As had happened in Canada, missionaries taught Alaskan women to spin and knit, and these women showed remarkable ability in mastering the crafts. Knitting socks, long johns, and undershirts for foreigners proved to be a very profitable cash business, an additional source of revenue required to smooth the Native people's transition into the twentieth century.

Knitting gave Alaskan Native women financial independence and a way to support their families while European colonialism hammered their traditional societies. Knitting literally held the tribes together—it purled and stitched its members to one another, protected their communal spirit, and maintained their traditions through the harsh journey of modernization. Women were able to knit to make money while traveling to fish camps and berry-picking areas in the summer, while preserving food for the coming winter each fall, and while caring for young children or elders throughout the year. Often working in cooperative knitting groups, these women were stitched together, and for that reason, despite enormous change, their communities re-mained whole.

On a flight from Los Angeles to Seattle, I sat next to a young Alaskan Native man. He told me that he and one of his siblings had been raised by his grandparents, who lived in a village near the one where his parents resided. Two of his siblings had stayed with his parents. I asked him how he felt about being separated from Mum and Dad, and he said that in his culture, the extended family is regarded as the parents, so he was not traumatized by being separated from his mother and father, and he did not feel deprived when he moved to live with his grandparents.

His extended family also shared their earnings. He told me that most of the women knit for money to contribute to the family income. His grandmother, who he said was in her nineties, had learned how to knit as a child from a Russian woman and had taught all her daughters and granddaughters. They knitted for a co-op, Oomingmak, the largest in Alaska.

I looked it up and was impressed by its history and knitted production. Oomingmak was created by a visionary entrepreneur from Vermont, John Teal, who believed that musk ox, large mammals resembling true oxen but more closely related to goats and genetically tied by a prehistoric ancestor that survived the last ice age, could be domesticated to produce wool. After running an experimental farm in Vermont for a decade, Teal moved to Alaska to develop a yarn and knitted products company for tourists. By 1968, the project was a success, and Oomingmak Musk Ox Producer's Co-operative was incorporated in 1970.

The musk ox has long, soft hair, which sheds naturally in the spring. The wool from the undercoat is collected by combing the animal; in the old days, the raw fiber was pulled away from the skin of the animal by hand. Musk ox wool is known as qiviut, a very special type of yarn that resembles cashmere. It is soft, warm, and waterproof, and can withstand temperature shock and agitation without shrinking or fulling. For decades, knitting beautiful qiviut outfits and lace has helped Alaskan Native families keep their refrigerators full and the principle of sharing alive.

Each member of the Oomingmak cooperative pays a two-dollar annual fee, and in exchange they are not charged for yarn, which is provided at the co-op's expense. All knitters have to do is buy their knitting needles. Because Oomingmak's members

are scattered across Alaska and traveling costs are prohibitive, all communication, delivery, and payments take place by mail.

"The knitters are paid by the stitch. Each project has a specific number of stitches cast on and a specific number of rows to knit, so the total can easily be calculated. The actual price per stitch changes over time with inflation but the goal is to give the knitters a fair price, while keeping the cost of the finished items at a price that will not make them seem unreasonable to tourists. At the end of the year, any profit is distributed to the knitters, with each receiving a percentage based on the number of items they knit during the year."

Discovering how knitting has given hope to the Alaskan Natives in a traumatic transition helps me believe that I will also be able to navigate my dramatic present and adapt to a different life. I will reach a safe shore, a place where I can begin a new journey, but I am not yet out of the woods. My peaceful lake house has been sold; in a month, I will pack my things and put them in storage. My books will be boxed and locked in a dark place and I will miss their smile every morning. My yarns, and my grandmother's shining metal needles, will also end up in storage; I will carry with me a small bag with whatever I will be knitting the day I leave and nothing else.

Change is always traumatic. However, it can ultimately be positive, despite what is lost. My good friend the Franciscan monk suggested I spend the summer traveling and observing the world, possibly with a small, half-empty suitcase, so I can bring back exotic yarn. "Be a cosmopolitan nomad for a while," he said, smiling. Why not? Yesterday I bought an around-the-world ticket. I will travel to visit friends in different countries and clear my mind. I have the luxury of an opportunity the Alaskan Native women did not have. As I sat down to plan my itinerary, I realized that knitting is once again guiding me. I want to go to New Zealand and Tasmania, places where I know I can find beautiful yarn and patterns, to Finland, to Iceland, and I want to visit Mongolia, the land of one of the last nomadic tribes.

A couple of years ago, I met an Asian American woman named Nancy Johnson when she came to do an interview at the BBC World Service radio program *Weekend*, on which I am sometimes a guest commentator. Johnson walked into the studio carrying a variety of beautiful, soft woolen fabrics from Tengri, a luxury fashion company she owns that produces men's knitwear, carpets, and soft furniture made with yak fiber from Mongolia. During the program, she explained that the yak is an ancient long-haired bovid that lives in the Himalayan region of the Indian subcontinent, on the Tibetan Plateau, in Mongolia, and in Russia. Nancy buys the yak fiber from nomadic families, has it spun and knitted in Yorkshire and Scotland, and sells the products worldwide. An interesting combination, I thought, which reminded me of the commercial loop between the raw materials from the American colonies and the textile industry of the Midlands in England during the Industrial Revolution. But, as Johnson pointed out, in her business model, there is no exploitation; on the contrary, what Tengri has done is revitalize two sectors in decline—nomadic sheep farming in Mongolia, and the British textile industry—by sharing the profits of her company with them.

Talking with Nancy led me to learn a lot more about life in Mongolia. In the last decade, traditional Mongolian nomadic life has come under threat from Western civilization and climate change, a powerful double whammy. Mongolia may be an example of both our pastoral past and a climatic dystopian future.

For millennia, in the steppe and in the Gobi Desert, men have lived a symbiotic existence with their herds of sheep, horses, cattle, goats, camels, and yaks, depending on one another for survival in a deeply hostile environment. Nomadic families guide the animals for thousands of miles to different pastures, sometimes moving six times per year. They pack and unpack their belongings to look after the herds, which are their livelihood. Nomadic pastoralism has allowed the Mongols to exploit the scarce resources of the land, which are insufficient to sustain a human and herbivore population for an entire year. As in the Iraqi desert, the key to survival has been to migrate from pasture to pasture.

Today, nomadic pastoralism in Mongolia rests on an extremely delicate equilibrium. A very cold winter, which generally follows a summer drought, could wipe out entire herds. In 2010, eight million animals died during one of the coldest winters in modern history. Since that year, Mongolia has suffered a few more extremely cold winters. With their herd gone, a nomadic family's sustenance economy implodes, leaving them destitute and forcing people to find jobs in overcrowded and smoke-filled cities working for the booming mining industry. Due to climate change, over the last thirty years a quarter of Mongolia has turned to desert and two thousand rivers have dried up. The country is on the cusp of an irreversible change.

Through all this change, Mongolian nomadic women have been spinning and knitting the wool and fiber from their herds to clothe and house their tribes. Mongolia produces two types of very valuable yarns: cashmere from goats, and yak fiber from yaks, which traditionally has been used to make felt for the yurts in which the nomads live, while cashmere has been knitted into garments to keep them warm. Mongolia produces about a fifth of the global supply of raw cashmere. At about $45 per kilogram of raw material, it is a reliable source of income for nomadic herders, bolstering traditional lifestyles threatened by rapid urbanization. In fact, the ratio of goats to people in the country has quadrupled since the fall of Communism, and now stands at around six to one.

Producing and selling cashmere, however, has been a mixed blessing for the struggling economy of nomadic families. Though the cash has kept many afloat during hard times, the proliferation of cashmere herds has depleted the pastures. Cashmere goats pluck out grass with its roots, which prevents it from growing back. The desertification in Mongolia has been caused in part by the increase in people keeping goats to supply the global cashmere demand. Industrialization and modernization risk turning Mongolia into a wasteland, a terrifying omen for our planet.

When Nancy Johnson was confronted with these facts, she was shocked. She knew that Mongolia supplied the luxury industry with cashmere and decided to investigate how to help people prevent the damage caused by this industry. She reached out to friends in fashion and came up with the idea of yak knitwear. "Yak fiber is as warm and soft as cashmere; it's also organic, hypoallergenic, antibacterial, and supports livelihoods. It's a miracle fiber. And it's machine washable!" Johnson told me. "Yaks also don't damage the environment the way goats do."

Unlike cashmere goats, yaks only eat the grass stalks, leaving the roots in the ground, which allows the grass to grow back. Johnson describes yaks as lawnmowers: they do not damage the ground, they only cut the grass. Interestingly, like musk oxen, yaks naturally shed their fur in the summer, so it is easy and ecologically friendly to collect their fiber.

Tengri is not a co-op like Oomingmak in Alaska; however, its business model is also constructed around the concept of profit sharing. Tengri pays a premium price for the yak fibers and supplies a deposit for each family in the co-op to put against the cost of feeding and tending the yaks. This model has been very successful, and today, the number of Mongolian yak herds raised for wool has increased exponentially, offering an ecological alternative to cashmere. Companies like Tengri and co-ops like Oomingmak in Alaska are instruments to help traditional communities weather the inevitable transition toward modernity without abandoning the principles of sharing and preserving the environment.

Knitting and economics have forged an alliance throughout the centuries and have provided a safety net for women and men while they were living through dramatic change, but there is less and less space for traditional societies and values in our world. Land degra-

dation, climate change, pollution, and waste are poisoning our planet, hindering sustainability. Corruption and greed erode social cohesion and foster inequality, threatening the communal fabric that holds us together.

As we enter a difficult future of new challenges, knitting can forge an alliance with politics, stitch the fractures, rebuild the bridges, clean the polluted air, sanitize the water, and bring back socialization. Can an ancient craft fight climatic Armageddon and political dystopia? Urban knitters and yarn bombers believe it can.

For over a decade, men and women have been getting together in urban areas to knit in protest against environmental degradation. From 2006 to 2007, the London-based group I Knit worked with WaterAid on a project called "Knit a River." Their aim was to draw people's attention to the one billion people in the world who do not have access to clean water. Volunteers worldwide knitted about one hundred thousand patches to form the knitted river. According to I Knit's website, during that event the river was "draped like a waterfall from the roof of the National Theatre on London's South Bank," and made for "a spectacular sight!"

In Canada, the Rock Vandals have used yarn bombing to voice their concern about the danger that the oil industry poses to the environment, but they have also yarn-bombed trees, lampposts, and pillars along the roads to bring some color to the bleakness of winter in the Far North.

Guerrilla knitting has offered a peaceful channel to protest bad politics. In August 2016, on the anniversary of the detonation of the first nuclear bomb in Japan, Wool Against Weapons knit a seven-mile-long scarf that connected AWE Aldermaston and AWE Burghfield, nuclear arms manufacturers in the UK. In Germany, the duo Strick & Liesel (a play on *strickliesel*, the German name for a knitting Nancy, a children's toy used to learn how to knit) started the Fluffy Throw-Up project, a uniquely soft and nonviolent form of protest against nuclear power. Their yellow-and-black logo is placed on trees, streetlamps, bridge bannisters, and pillars in cities throughout Germany.

Yarn bombing is also used to breach gender and racial barriers. In Chile, Hombres Tejedores (Male Knitters) knit in public to break down traditional male and female stereotypes. In Reykjavík, Yarnstormers cover street poles and trees with knitted rainbows for the annual Gay Pride festival, while dressing public statues at night with colorful knitwear.

In 2014, after the fatal shooting of Michael Brown in Ferguson, Missouri, Taylor Payne and CheyOnna Sewell, two political activists, formed the Yarn Mission, described as a knitting collective to fight racial injustice through community. The quiet, safe setting of a knitting circle helps people talk about their traumatic experiences and begin to heal together.

There are hundreds of thousands of similar guerrilla-knitting initiatives across the world. They all require mobilization, participation, organization, planning, and a clear vision of the future. Protest knitting is the modern equivalent of the traditional political grassroots movements, such as the suffrage, civil rights, women's liberation, and freedom of speech movements. Yarn bombers are activists, people who get out of their

homes to meet with others and act together. The Pussyhat Project got women to knit pink hats to wear at the Women's March in January 2017; it motivated them to knit and march in the streets, creating a sea of woolly hats, many knit by volunteers (see pattern at the end of the book). Even when the mobilization is not directly linked to a political event, guerrilla knitters such as Knittami in Italy, a yarn-bombing group whose slogan is "Cover the city with wool," are old-style activists. They organize, collaborate, and demonstrate in public places to spread their message of hope and social change.

Occupy Wall Street, the Indignados Movement in Spain, the Umbrella Revolution in Hong Kong—all have come and gone, bursts of political activism that have burned out quickly like candles. But yarn bombing is still going strong. Urban knitting is a long-term global phenomenon, popping up in Alaska, New Zealand, Sweden, the United States, everywhere. So why do we know so little about the knitting revolution? The answer is simple: the media is uninterested in a peaceful, silent, and long-term protest movement mostly created by women, just as it was not interested in the knitting activity of the hippie movement. There is nothing sensational about yarn bombing the interior of a bus in Reykjavík, a winter park in Anchorage, or the Embarcadero waterfront in San Francisco. No one shouts slogans, no one gets hurt; woolly activism is almost cozy. However, the real protest is hidden behind the knitted items superimposed upon our environment; the revolutionary message is encoded in the mass mobilization to knit for a cause alone at home, but also together, in knitting circles. Behind the yarn bombing there are the guerrilla knitters, people committed to a cause, people who have ideals, people who care for one another and who work together to create something new.

Their personal contribution may be as small as one of the knitted flowers attached to the naked branches of winter trees in Anchorage parks or one of the five thousand poppies knit annually to remember fallen soldiers, initially those of World War II, but now for those who have served in all wars and conflicts (see pattern at the end of the book). But these contributions are not insignificant. *I have not given up, I will not give up*—that is the knitter's spirit. This is what my grandmother taught me: the job of a knitter is never done; there is always another pattern and new yarn to knit for those we love. Creating a better world, like knitting, has no end, it is an endless effort and at the same time a necessity, like breathing.

We are all interlinked, the rich and the poor, the citizens and the migrants. We are part of the same yarn and pattern. This is the true power of knitting, the ultimate metaphor of life: each of us is a stitch and a purl of global society, and we are stronger together.

All You Need Is Love

I am at LAX, waiting to board the first flight of my around-the-world trip. I have no home now; the house in London is rented, the one in the US has been sold, and all my furniture and belongings are in storage on two separate continents, including my beloved books. I am traveling with two suitcases, one for winter and one for summer, a knitting bag with several balls of yarn, and my laptop. This is all I have with me; this is all I need, for now. I also no longer have a husband, and no children to look after—they have grown up and live in different cities and continents; for the first time in forty years, I am totally on my own. For months I have feared this moment, anticipating that it would be sad and emotionally challenging, even tearful. This is why I am carrying my knitting bag with me, for comfort and to help me heal.

Some time ago, I came across an amazing story of knitting

and healing. An Englishwoman, Clare Young, had developed post-traumatic stress disorder, depression, and anxiety after the death of her husband. Her psychologist suggested that she learn to knit. With the help of some friends, she yarn-bombed a tree at the hospice in Cheltenham, Gloucester, to thank the staff who had cared for her husband during the last stage of his illness. This is why she also knit look-alike dolls of the doctors, nurses, housekeeping staff—anyone who had interacted with him—and placed them under the tree on a blanket. When I saw the pictures of Clare's yarn-bomb installation, I thought the look-alike knitted dolls were having a picnic under the tree, enjoying a beautiful English spring day in the garden of the hospice. It was a joyful image, drenched in love and happiness, a celebration of life.

Clare did such an amazing job that photos of her yarn bombing became a sort of sensation online, and some even called her the Gloucester Banksy, after the elusive street artist. The response to her project so moved her that she was inspired to ask people to knit small woolen hearts in memory of their loved ones, hearts that she would place in a knitted healing garden at the hospice (see pattern at the end of the book). She posted her request on Facebook, and soon had received more than 52,000 hearts from 450 knitters all over the world. Many sent their knitted hearts with moving notes about lost loved ones. Soon after, she launched another appeal, in which she asked people to donate their leftover wool and yarn they were not using so that she could carry on knitting flowers, pots, and plants for another healing garden, this time for the Royal Horticultural Society.

Among the people who heard about her was Ian, a man who had lost his wife a year earlier. His wife had been a knitter, and she had left behind a lot of yarn. When he saw Clare on TV, he was touched by her initiative and impressed by her determination. He decided to get in touch with her to donate his wife's wool. They met, and eventually fell in love.

The yarn that Ian's wife had not been able to knit was the thread that brought Ian to Clare, and Clare's celebration of the love and devotion for her husband provided the pattern to stitch their lives together. As Clare knit her grief away, Ian did the same by providing her the yarn to knit, and together, one stitch at a time, one knitted flower after another, love blossomed, filling the emptiness left by their loss.

Today Clare continues to knit flowers, plants, and gardens for charity, and Ian, as a devoted husband, supports her in her mission. They are happy, living together surrounded by the beautiful knitted vegetation she produces. In an interview with the BBC, they talk about their deceased spouses with fondness; they have not forgotten them but have overcome their deaths and begun living again.

Unlike Clare, I have not been traumatized by death, but I am also in need of healing; like her, I have chosen knitting, and in my case, writing about knitting, to help me recover. During the last six months, I have unraveled forty years of existential knitting, I have unwound most of the fabric of my adult life with my own hands. Though I have done this using the wisdom of my grandmother, with courage and determination as a good knitter would, the experience has been traumatic. As I was pulling free row after row of stitches, I traveled in reverse through my life, revisiting emotional landscapes I had left behind years ago and forgotten about. Navigating through my memories, I took great care not to cut the yarn, not to disconnect, to accept and learn from my mistakes, but at times I was forced to sever the strand: a stitch had been made within the fibers of the yarn and could not be worked free, or the wool had thickened through several washings and had bonded two stitches together, turning them into a tiny mass of felt. Each time this happened, I feared I would lose the thread of my life and be unable to reuse the yarn without inserting knots, ugly bumps in between the stitches of the fabric. I was afraid my new life would end up being worse than my previous one.

My grandmother's teaching helped me overcome those fears: as she so often said, you must do your best to unravel the yarn smoothly and use your skill to hide the knots when you reknit it. I hope her love and wisdom will continue guiding me when I begin reknitting the old, unraveled balls of yarn I now carry around the world in my knitting bag.

I was not the only person I knew boarding a plane in the United States for a foreign country in order to have a life reboot. Maria's son had flown away a week earlier, never to return. He had lived in the US nearly all his life; he was five when he came to the country with his mother and sister on a tourist visa. He won several prestigious scholarships, which had allowed him to study in the best schools of the country. He was married, had a very good job, owned a house, a boat, two dogs, and a car, and his wife worked as an accountant. But at age thirty-nine, he did not have a US passport. Nobody knows why the renewal of his two-year work permit, a routine administrative procedure, was denied. Possibly it was a computer error. But the immigration lawyer he consulted ruled out an appeal because it might have resulted in his being detained for up to two years, waiting with illegal immigrants for a court decision.

When Maria was told that her beloved son had to leave the US, she was devastated. Just as I had done when my life began to unravel, her son frantically evaluated different scenarios in which he might return to North America. His best chance seemed to be to enroll in an MBA program in Canada and apply for Canadian citizenship, a process that could take five years. Five years without being able to see his mother, because she cannot leave the US; she also has a work permit visa but neither a passport nor a green card. And of course he will never be allowed to enter the US again.

Spring for Maria and myself was a time of planning, testing, and scheming to find the best solution to our problems. We cried a lot, but we also comforted each other. What kept us going, through the bad news and the setbacks, was knitting, and caring for each other. Every evening we sat together with our needles and yarn as we reported to each other the news of the day. Sometimes I showed her videos of knitting stories I'd come across or patterns I had found during my research, or I read aloud passages I had written for this book. Often she brought knitting books from the library for me to look at. We tested new patterns, so caught up in our activity that sometimes we knit until the small hours of the morning. Because neither of us could sleep for long, knitting filled the empty hours of our insomnia.

The day her son left, Maria did not go to the airport to say goodbye. It would have been too painful for both of them. Instead, she came to see me to discuss the plan she had finalized:

she would work for another two years, save enough money, and then leave the US. From her native country, she could travel to visit her son in Canada twice a year, until they could be reunited for good. She was not sad, she did not cry; she was excited about the future. Her enthusiasm made her look younger, stronger, successful. She was no longer afraid to redesign her life and start all over again at the age of sixty-four.

When I was a teenager and I first heard Paul McCartney sing, "Will you still love me when I'm sixty-four?" from the famous Beatles song "When I'm Sixty-Four," I thought that sixty-four was a very, very old age. But now that I have reached that age, I feel younger than I did when I was in my fifties, or my forties. Like Maria, I am experiencing a surge of energy because I have a plan, and I have a strong curiosity about the future.

Has all this turmoil been a blessing in disguise? Have I really lost everything—a husband, a very comfortable life, two beautiful houses, a prominent place among the society of the wealthy? Or could it be the opposite: that I have gained my freedom, that what I thought I had knit for forty years was not a security blanket but a straitjacket? As I undid things throughout my financial and emotional ordeal, unraveling the metaphorical yarn of the sleeves, of the back, of the strings that had locked my arms around my waist, I unloaded heavy existential burdens, emotional weight that had prevented me from soaring, from being myself. I was freeing a woman from a character she had played for decades, from a made-up life she had believed was better than her reality, a woman who had knit the wrong pattern, one too constricting for her, yet one she'd pretended was perfect. And I was able to do this thanks to the love and knitting legacy of my grandmother.

PATTERNS

Pussy Power Hat

(see pages 8, 155)

SIZE

Small (Medium/Large)

MATERIALS

1 skein Malabrigo Worsted
(210 yards per 100 g) in Fucsia
(any shade of worsted weight pink yarn will do)

1 pair US size 8 / 5mm needles

MEASUREMENTS

Gauge: 18 sts x 23 rows = 4" / 10cm in Stockinette stitch

Finished size: 9 ¼" / 23.5cm (11"/ 28cm) wide and 14 ¾" / 37.5cm
(17 ¼"/ 43.8cm) long before seaming

STITCHES

Stockinette stitch: Knit RS rows, purl WS rows.

PATTERN

CO 42 (50) sts. Leave a long tail for seaming.

Rib: K1 *k2, p2; repeat from * to last st, p1.

Work Rib for 3 ¼" / 8.25cm (4 ¼" / 10.8cm) ending with a WS row.

Work in St st until piece measures 11 ½" / 29.2cm (13" / 33cm)
from cast-on edge, ending with a WS row.

Begin Rib on RS row: P1 *p2, k2; repeat from * to last st, k1.

Work Rib for 3 ¼" / 8.25cm (4 ¼" / 10.8cm), until piece measures
14 ¾" / 37.5cm (17 ¼"/ 43.8cm) from cast-on edge.

With RS facing, bind off all stitches. Cut yarn, leaving a long tail for seaming.

Fold hat in half and sew each side seam. Weave in loose ends.

Put on the hat, and the cat ears will appear!

Wig Hat

(see page 29)

SIZE

One size (adult)

MATERIALS

Red Heart 100% acrylic (5 oz./140 g) in purple

1 pair US size 8 / 5mm needles

5 US size 8 / 5mm double-pointed needles, or two US size 8 / 5mm circular needles (any length)

4 stitch markers, 2 each of 2 different colors

Tapestry needle

MEASUREMENTS

Gauge: 28 sts x 22 rows = 4" / 10cm in 2x2 Rib (unstretched)

Finished size: 8" / 20cm wide at widest point and 11" / 28cm long when flat (unstretched)

STITCHES

2x2 Rib

Row 1 (RS): K3, [p2, k2] to last st, k1.

Row 2 (WS): P3, [k2, p2] to last st, p1.

PATTERN

Wig

Using straight needles or one set of circular needles, cast on 96 sts.

Work in 2x2 Rib until the piece is as long as the distance between your eyebrow and the bottom of your chin (about 6 ½" / 16.5cm), ending with a WS row.

If more length in the main body of the wig is desired, work more rows at this point.

Next row (RS): Work as before, but sl first and last sts.

Bangs

With RS facing and using Backward Loop Cast-On, loosely cast on 32 sts.

NOTE: The Backward Loop Cast-On allows for plenty of stretch.

Divide sts onto dpns or circular needles and join to work in the round with RS of wig facing out, being careful not to twist sts.

The first st will be a p; follow 2x2 Rib pattern after that.

Work in 2x2 Rib for 10 rows. If more length in the bangs is desired, work more rows at this point.

NOTE: The extra stitches that were at the beginning and end of the work up to this point become part of purl ribs where the bangs join— see diagram A on page 172.

Decreases

Using diagram B on page 173 as a guide, rearrange sts on needles and pm. When placing markers, begin counting from the center front of the bangs, which falls in the center of a purl rib.

NOTE: Diagram B shows marker placement for both double-pointed and circular needles.

PATTERNS

171

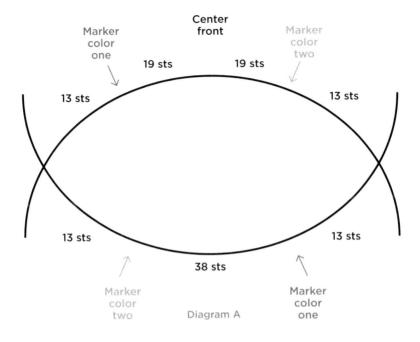

Center front

Marker color one

Marker color two

19 sts   19 sts

13 sts   13 sts

13 sts   13 sts

38 sts

Marker color two

Marker color one

Diagram A

NOTE: Decreases will be worked identically at the front and back of the wig. Markers have been placed one stitch away from decreases instead of directly next to decreases for ease of working.

Decrease Round: Begin decrease round by working decreases over bangs. *Work in 2x2 rib as set to marker color 1, sm, k1, ssk, 2x2 rib as set to 3 sts before marker color 2, k2tog, k1, sm; repeat from * every round until 6 sts remain between markers.

Work to marker color 1 (right edge of bangs).

Next Round: *Sm, k1, ssk, k2tog, k1, sm, [p2tog, k2] to 2 sts before next marker, p2tog; repeat from * once.

Remove st marker, k1, sl1. Transfer first half of the work (between center front and center back) to one dpn or circular needle, removing st markers. Transfer second half of the work to a second needle and cut yarn, leaving a 24" / 60cm length for binding off.

Finishing

Carefully flip work inside out in preparation for working a 3-needle bind-off from the WS.

Work 3-needle bind-off tightly. (A crochet hook works well in place of a third needle.)

Weave in ends and turn right side out.

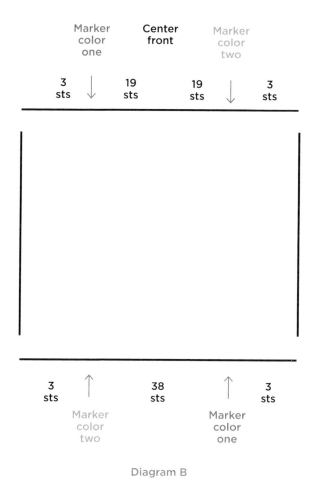

Diagram B

World War I and II Service Socks

MATERIALS

One 4 ounce ball P.K. Victory Service Yarn

Needles for average knit – No. 11.

(see page 51)

Needles for tight knit – No. 10.

Needles for loose knit – No. 12.

PATTERN

Cast on loosely 60 stitches (20-20-20).
Rib 4 inches, 2 plain, 2 purl.

Knit plain 7 or 8 inches according to length of leg desired.

Heel

Knit plain 28 stitches on to one needle, turn, purl back these 28 stitches, turn, knit plain.

Repeat these 2 rows (always slipping the first stitch) 11 times (12 in all) or 24 rows. Having the inside of the heel toward you, purl 15 stitches, purl 2 together, purl 1.

Turn, k4, k2tog, k1.

Turn, p5, p2tog, p1.

Turn, k6, k2tog, k1.

Turn, p7, p2tog, p1.

Turn, k8, k2tog, k1.

Turn, p9, p2tog, p1.

Turn, k10, k2tog, k1.

Turn, p11, p2tog, p1.

Turn, k12, k2tog, k1.

Turn, p13, p2tog, p1.

Turn, k14, k2tog, k1.

Pick up and knit the 12 stitches down the side of heel piece.

Knit 2 stitches off the front needle.

Knit 28 stitches off of the front needle on to one needle, the last 2 stitches knit onto third needle, on which pick up and knit the 12 stitches at other side of heel piece.

Divide the heel stitches on the 2 side needles, and knit the right around again to the center of the heel.

First needle: k to within 3 stitches of the front end of side needle, k2tog, k1.

Front needle, knit.

Third needle, k1, k2tog, k to end of needle.

Reduce in this way every other row until there are 56 stitches on needles (front needle 28, side needles 14 each).

Knit plain until the foot, from the pack of the heel measures:

To obtain different sizes:

8 inches for size 10

9 inches for size 11

10 inches for size 12

Toe (combination)

On front needle k2, k2tog, k to within 4 stitches from end of needle.

K2tog, k2.

On first side k2, k2tog, k to end of needle.

K to within 4 stitches from end of second side needle, k2tog, k2, k around plain.

Repeat these two rows until there are 10 stitches on front needle and 5 on each of side needles. Now slip stitches from one side needle to the other, making 10 stitches on 2 needles. Break yarn, leaving a tail of about 10 inches. You will now graft the toe using the Kitchener stitch.

Thread the tail into a darning needle. Put through the first stitch on the front needle, as if for purling, but do not take the stitch off. Then put the darning needle through the first stitch on the back needle, as if for purling, and take off.

*Put the needle through next stitch on back needle, as if for knitting, and do not take it off. Then place it through the first stitch on front needle, as if for knitting, and slip off. Then through the second stitch on front needle, as if for purling, and do not take off. Then through the first stitch on back needle, as if for purling, and take off.

Repeat from * until all the stitches are worked off.

NOTE: Each stitch must be gone through twice, except the first and last on the back needles. Always keep the yarn under the knitting needles. In finishing off the end of yarn, run yarn once down through the toe so as not to make a ridge or lump.

Finishing

Put on sock stretchers of correct size and press with damp towel and warm iron. Do not hang up to dry.

Sew size label in each sock.

Tie two socks together.

Phrygian Cap

(see page 57)

SIZE

One size (adult)

MATERIALS

Cap: 8-ply (DK) yarn in red (about 50g)

Rosette: 8-ply (DK) yarn in blue, white, and red

US size 9 / 5.5mm circular needles or double-pointed needles

2 stitch markers

PATTERN

Hat

Cast on 80 sts.

Knit until the work measures 6 ½" / 16.5cm.

NOTE: This is based on personal preference; my brim is just about 2″ folded up and was added at the end.

Decrease and Shaping

Pm to divide the sts in half (40, 40).

repeat within first half [second half].

Round 1: *K3, k2tog* [knit].

Round 2: Knit.

Round 3: *K2, k2tog* [knit].

Round 4: Knit.

Round 5: *K1, k2tog* [knit].

Round 6: Knit.

Round 7: *K2tog* [k8, k2tog, k20, ssk, k8].

Round 8: Knit.

Round 9: *K2tog* [k6, k2tog, k22, ssk, k6].

Round 10: Knit.

Round 11: *K2tog* [k4, k2tog, k24, ssk, k4].

Round 12: Knit.

Round 13: *K2tog* [k2, k2tog, k26, ssk, k2]; 33 sts remain.

Knit for about 3 ½" / 9cm, trying hat on periodically and folding up the back to check length for preference.

Finishing

When desired size is reached, [K3, k2tog] for one round.

Draw through remaining sts and tie off.

Fold up brim and sew loosely.

NOTE: The back will fold up and stay up on its own, but I would recommend sewing or pinning it because it looks hilariously ridiculous if it falls.

Rosette

Cast on 52 sts in white.

Rows 1–3: Work 2x2 Rib in red.

Rows 4–6: Work 2x2 Rib in white.

Row 7: Work 2x2 Rib in blue.

Row 8: In blue, k2tog across row. Where there is an odd number of stitches, knit last st.

Cut yarn and thread through remaining sts. Pull up to form rosette.

Sew rosette to side of hat.

Unisex Vest

The vest has a negative ease; the stretchiness
makes the ribbing more prominent.
It is also short-waisted, like many vintage
garments.

(see page 66)

Small/Medium (Large/Extra-
Large)

MATERIALS

10-ply yarn suitable for US size 8 / 5mm needles in 3 colors
(about 250m of each)

US size 6 / 4mm needles (preferably circular)

US size 8 / 5mm needles (preferably circular)

STITCHES

1x1 Rib

1) K1, p1.

2) Work sts as they appear.

3x1 Rib

1) K3, p1.

2) Work sts as they appear.

MEASUREMENTS

Finished size: 13 ¼/16" (16 ½"/20") / 34/41cm (42/51cm) wide, 19"
(21 ½") / 48cm (54cm) long; 8 to 8 ¼" / 20 to 21cm armhole

The three colors are alternated every 4 rows, always in the same sequence (1, 2, 3) = 12 rows, followed through all the work.

Back

Cast on 80 (100) sts with size 6 / 4mm needles (for long tail cast-on).

Work in 1x1 Rib for 2 color sequence = 24 rows.

Change to size 8 / 5mm needles.

Work for 6 (7) color repetitions = 72 (84) rows

Armhole decrease: Bind off 8 (12) sts at beginning of next 2 rows, then decrease 2 sts at beginning of next 2 rows, then 1 st at beginning of next 2 rows.*

Continue with the remaining sts until you get 4 color sequences starting from the start of the armhole and 2 rows with color 1.

Bind off loosely.

Front

Work as Back until *.

Continue with remaining sts for 12 rows (1 color sequence) from armhole.

Neck Shaping: K32 (40), bind off 16 (20) for neck, knit to end of row.

Working on the right shoulder sts, decrease 2 sts at neck edge on next row and 1 sts on next 2 rows.

Continue with remaining sts until you get 4 color sequences starting from the start of the armhole and 2 rows with color 1.

Bind off loosely.

Finishing and Edges

Sew shoulder seams together.

Neckline: Using size 6 / 4mm circular needles, pick up the sts around the neck, then work 5 rounds of 1x1 Rib.

Bind off loosely.

Armhole: Using size 6 / 4mm circular needles, pick up the sts around the armhole, then work 5 rounds of 1x1 Rib.

Bind off loosely.

Bikini

SIZE

European size 40–42, US size 10–12

MATERIALS

4-ply cotton yarn (better if elasticized; 50 g = 100 m) in 2 colors: 2 balls color A, 1 ball color B

US size 2.5 / 3mm circular needle

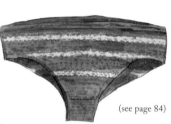

STITCHES

Moss Stitch

Rows 1 and 2: *Knit one, purl one. Repeat from * across.

Rows 3 and 4: *Purl one, knit one. Repeat from * across.

(see page 84)

PATTERN

Bikini Bottom

NOTE: This item is knitted from the bottom up.

Cast on 41 sts with color A.

Work in St st:

1) K1, k2tog, knit to last 3 sts, sl1, psso, k1. 2 sts dec'd.

2) Purl.

Repeat twice with color A, then repeat steps 1 and 2 with color B.

Resume with color A, repeating steps 1 and 2 until you have 15 sts on the needle.

Work for 4 ¼" / 11cm (gusset).

Start to increase for the back:

1) K1, M1, knit to last st, M1, k1. 2 sts inc'd.

2) P1, M1, purl to last st, M1, p1. 2 sts inc'd.

Continue until you have 63 sts, ending on a WS row, then repeat steps 1 and 2 with color B.

Resume with color A, repeating steps 1 and 2 until you have 71 sts on the needle.

Begin working in the round, joining front and back.

With RS of work in front of you, cast on 15 sts, pick up the 41 sts of the front, cast on 15 sts.

Work in circular St st:

1) 1 row color A.

2) 2 rows color B.

3) 8 rows color A.

4) 2 rows color B.

5) 4 rows color A.

Work 4 rows color A in moss stitch.

Cast off and weave in loose ends.

Bra

Prepare an I-cord about 16"/ 40cm long.

From here, work back and forth in St st, taking as a basis the 3 sts mounted for the I-cord; every 8 rows with color A, work 2 rows with color B.

1) K1, M1, k1, M1, k1. 2 sts inc'd.

2) Purl.

Continue until you have 41 stitches.

Begin to shape the cup:

1) K1, M1, k18, sk2po, k18, M1, k1 (no increase).

2) Purl.

Repeat steps 1 and 2 to make the second cup.

Begin working the edge for the underbust cord:

1) Knit.

2) Knit.

3) *K1, k2tog, yo; repeat from * to last 2 sts, k2.

4) Knit.

Bind off and weave in loose ends.

Prepare a 47" / 120cm long I-cord and insert it through the holes at the base of the cups.

Rastafarian Hat

(see page 95)

One size (adult)

MATERIALS

1 ball each DROPS Polaris in
black, red, yellow, and green

7mm circular needle (32" / 80cm long)

Stitch marker

US size G-6 / 4mm crochet hook

Tapestry needle

STITCHES

1x1 Rib: *K1, p1; repeat from * to end.

Use magic loop technique for decreasing.

PATTERN

Hat

Cast on 56 sts with the preferred method using black yarn and join to
knit in the round, being careful not to twist sts. Pm.

Work 7 rows in 1x1 Rib.

Work 3 rounds:

1) Knit.

2) Knit.

3) K2, M1 (picking up the yarn before the next st), and repeat for the
round to marker (84 sts).

Continue on the 84 sts for 10 rounds in each color:

1) 10 rounds red.

2) 10 rounds yellow.

3) 10 rounds green.

Decrease in green:

1) K2tog to marker (42 sts).

2) K2tog to marker (21 sts).

Draw yarn through the remaining sts with a tapestry needle, tighten, and weave in ends.

Visor

Pick up 21 sts from the cast-on edge on WS of the hat (starting with a purl). Continue in 1x1 Rib, matching the sts from the hat.

Decrease:

1) K2tog to last st, k1.

2) K2tog to last st, k1.

3) K2tog.

Draw yarn through the remaining sts with a tapestry needle, tighten, and weave in ends.

Using crochet hook, work in sl st around the visor
(to keep the visor stretched; otherwise, it tends to shrink).

Cut yarn and weave in loose ends.

Rib Stitch Poppy

MATERIALS

8-ply (DK) yarn in black and red

US size 5 / 3.75mm needles (Depending on how tight your knitting is, you might want to use needles one size larger or smaller.)

Tapestry needle

Decorative button, if desired

Safety clasp pin back

PATTERN

Cast on 52 sts in red.

Rows 1–6: Work in 2x2 rib.

Rows 7–9: K2tog across row. Where there is an odd number of sts, knit last st.

Cut yarn and thread through remaining sts. Pull up to form poppy. Stitch side seam. If using decorative button, attach to center.

NOTE: The last 3 rows can be done in black yarn to create the center of the poppy, but a button works equally well.

Attach pin to back of poppy.

Brain Hat

(see page 129)

SIZE

One size (adult)

MATERIALS

1 skein Bernat Giggles in purple

US size 8 / 5mm circular needles (16" / 40cm)

US size 8 / 5mm double-pointed needles

Tapestry needle

MEASUREMENTS

Gauge: 20 sts x 24 rows = 4" / 10cm

PATTERN

Cast on 76 sts.

Join for working in the round, being careful not to twist your sts.

Row 1: *K1, p1; repeat from * to end.

Rows 2 8: Repeat Row 1.

Rows 9–28: Knit.

Begin decreases:

Row 29: *K1, ssk, k14, k2tog; repeat from * to end (68 sts).

Row 30: Knit.

Row 31: *K1, ssk, k12, k2tog; repeat from * to end (60 sts).

Row 32: Repeat Row 30.

Row 33: *K1, ssk, k10, k2tog; repeat from * to end (52 sts).

Row 34: Repeat Row 30.

Row 35: *K1, ssk, k8, k2tog; repeat from * to end (44 sts).

Row 36: Repeat Row 30.

Row 37: *K1, ssk, k6, k2tog; repeat from * to end (36 sts).

Row 38: Repeat Row 30.

Row 39: *K1, ssk, k4, k2tog; repeat from * to end (28 sts).

Row 40: Repeat Row 30.

Row 41: *K1, ssk, k2, k2tog; repeat from * to end (20 sts). Switch to dpns, if needed.

Row 42: Repeat Row 30.

Row 43: *K2tog; repeat from * to end (10 sts).

Row 44: K1, k2tog to last st, k1 (6 sts).

Row 45: K2tog (3 sts).

Thread yarn through remaining sts, pull tight, and weave in loose ends.

NOTE: This pattern creates a cap that sits above the ears to represent the brain. If you would prefer a larger hat that covers the ears and would be suitable for winter, simply add more rows before decreasing until you reach your desired length.

Finishing

Cast on 5 sts with dpns.

Knit I-cord. You will need approx. 10 to 12' / 3 to 3.5m of I-cord per side of the cap. I recommend knitting approx. 6' / 2m, then starting to attach it to the hat without casting off from the needle. This will make the I-cord more manageable but still in one long piece.

Attach the I-cord to hat using whip stitch in a squiggly brainlike pattern. To attach, fold cap in half; this will help you create the hemispheres of the brain and not cross over onto the other side. **Just be careful not to sew your cap closed!** This is where you can get as creative as you like, making big and small swirls, squiggles, and loops. Do what you feel and get creative. Use your brain power.

Heart

MATERIALS

Merino yarn (can be made with any type or weight of yarn, taking care to maintain the proportion between height and width)

1 pair US size 8 / 5mm needles

Filler material (cotton, wool, etc.)

(see page 160)

MEASUREMENTS

Gauge: 17 sts x 22 rows = 4" / 10cm

STITCHES

Garter Stitch

Knit all rows. 1 ridge = 2 rows garter st.

Work sideways back and forth. When you finish, you will have one piece of knitting that you will fold in half, creating the two sides of the heart pillow.

PATTERN

Cast on 26 sts, leaving about 16" / 40cm yarn at the beginning.

Work in garter st until piece measures 1 ¼"/ 3cm.

On the next 2 rows, cast off 7 sts at the beginning of each row (14 sts).

Work in garter st for 1 ¼" / 3cm.

Cut the yarn, leaving about 16" / 40cm.

Pull yarn through last 12 sts and pull to tighten.

Fold in half and sew together at the top. Secure the thread.

Pull the cast-on thread through all the outermost sts and tighten.

Sew together down the side, while at the same time filling the heart with the stuffing.

ACKNOWLEDGMENTS

I wrote this book during the hardest time of my life. However, while researching and writing it, I experienced so much love and kindness and received so much unexpected support to make me overcome all my difficulties and look at life once again with hope.

My deepest thanks to:

Loretta Dal Pozzo and Oliver Balmelli, Giovanna Amato, Suzy and Mark Luben, Lesley and George Magnus, Vivian and David Ereira, Gaby Ereira, Silvia and Stefano Mazzola, Sarah Freeman, Kate Snell, Marianne Heier, Miriam Cosic, Barbara and Bruce Macevoy, Bonnie Hannigan and David Crow, Patricia Beck, Marisela, Emma Ulvaeus, Bjorn Axelsson, Angela Cook, Barbara Beattie, Lindsley and Stephen Robinson, Cristina Longati, Grazia Baravelli, Marcella Bernardini, Delia Zangelmi, Cristina De Pietro, Carlotta Borghi, Paolo and Alessandra Tosi, Scott Strellnauer, and many, many others. Thank you to Silvia Marazza and Helvia Persiani, and a special thanks to Muriel Mendoza for her amazing stories about knitting during World War II and meeting her husband. Thank you to Angelica and Vittorio Pignatti and Eleonor and Stephen Creaturo for caring about me.

Thank you to all the knitters, wool-shop owners, and assistants I met around the world during my research; your advice and wisdom has been extremely valuable.

As usual, my agents, Diana Finch and Marco Vigevani, believed in

my project and help me complete it; without their support and professional advice, this book could not have become a reality.

A special mention to Alessandra Olanow, the illustrator of this book.

A special thanks goes to my wonderful assistant, Federico Bastiani,
and to his wife, Laurel, who went the extra mile to support me; and to
Padre Emidio and Giuseppe Pasini for being there for me all the time.

BIBLIOGRAPHY

Korda, Holly. *The Knitting Brigades of World War I: Volunteers for Victory in America and Abroad*. Menlo Park, CA: New Enterprise, 2019.

Le Huche, Magali. *Hector, l'homme extraordinairement fort*. Paris: Didier Jeunesse, 2008.

Levine, Barbara. *People Knitting: A Century of Photographs*. New York: Princeton Architectural Press, 2016.

Lundberg, Anna-Karin. *Medieval-Inspired Knits: Stunning Brocade & Swirling Vine Patterns with Embellished Borders*. London: Trafalgar Square Books, 2013.

MacDonald, Anne L. *No Idle Hands: The Social History of American Knitting*. New York: Ballantine Books, 1990.

Matthews, Rachael. *The Mindfulness in Knitting: Meditations on Craft and Calm*. Brighton, UK: Leaping Hare Press, 2017.

Nargi, Lela. *Knitting Around the World: A Multistranded History of a Time-Honored Tradition*. London: Voyageur Press, 2011.

Nargi, Lela, ed. *Knitting Through It: Inspiring Stories for Times of Trouble*. London: Voyageur Press, 2008.

Rowlandson, Mary. *A Narrative of Captivity, Sufferings and Removes of Mrs. Mary Rowlandson*. Boston: Nathaniel Coverly, 1770.

Rutt, Richard. *A History of Hand Knitting*. Fort Collins, CO: Interweave Press, 1989.

Stoller, Debbie. *Stitch 'n Bitch: The Knitter's Handbook*. New York: Workman, 2004.

Strawn, Susan M. *Knitting America: A Glorious Heritage from Warm Socks to High Art*. London: Voyageur Press, 2011.

Warner, Geraldine. *Protest Knits: Got Needles? Get Knitting*. London: Herbert Press, 2017.

NOTES

Chapter Two: Opening the Yarn Cage

31. **a monthly series called True Stories Toronto:** https://www.youtube.com /watch?v=g5_cUvZErjU.

38. **curtail the colonies' economic growth:** In 1764, the British government enacted the Sugar Act; in 1765, the Stamp Act; in 1765, the Quartering Act; in 1767, the Townsend Acts (paint, tea, glass, and paper); in 1773, the Tea Act; and in 1774, the Coercive Acts. http://ww1centenary.oucs.ox.ac .uk/memoryofwar/crafts-craze-echoes-world-war-i-knitting-projects/.

Chapter Three: Knitting for the Revolution

71. **The G8 is a meeting:** https://www.indymedia.org.uk/en/2002/03/25858 .html.

Chapter Four: Feminism's Love-Hate Relationship with Yarn

81. **They did not know what was wrong with their lives:** *Makers: Women Who Make America*, "The Feminine Mystique," aired February 26, 2013, on PBS, https://www.pbs.org/video/makers-women-who-make-america -feminine-mystique/.

88. **True social change would only come:** Debbie Stoller, *Stitch 'n Bitch* (New York: Workman Publishing Company, 2004).

91. **It took him some time to gather the courage:** TrueExclusives, "Get to Know Brooklyn Boy Knits: | Viral Subway Knitter," uploaded April 23, 2018, https://www.youtube.com/watch?v=1Ssv3rZMzo4.

91. **Among these liberators are:** https://heavymetalknitting.fi/en/.

Chaper Five: Wool Is Cool

103. **Therapeutic knitting groups promote purpose:** Jill Riley, Betsan Corkhill, and Clare Morris, "The Benefits of Knitting for Personal and Social Wellbeing in Adulthood: Findings from an International Survey," *British Journal of Occupational Therapy* 76, no. 2 (February 15, 2013): 50–57, http://neurobiography.info/nb_article.php?article=35582.

110. **The grocer then resold the socks for 75 cents:** Macdonald, Anne. *No Idle Hands: The Social History of American Knitting* (New York: Ballantine Books, 1990).

113. **Some time ago, I came across a moving knitting story:** Kim Harris, "In a Knitting Club, I Found a Cure for Selfishness and Cynicism," *Globe and Mail*, January 17, 2016, https://www.theglobeandmail.com/life/facts-and -arguments/a-stitch-in-time/article28223076/.

116. **In 2017, Jayna Zweiman, cofounder of the Pussyhat Project:** Welcome Blanket On Call: Call to Action, https://www.welcomeblanket.org /oncall.

120. **While researching this book I came across WARM:** http://www.seam .org.au/warm.

128. **As we age, the more we use these connections:** Sarah McKay, "This Is Your Brain on Knitting," *Your Brain Health*, http://yourbrainhealth.com .au/brain-knitting/.

129. **In 2014, a group of knitters in Australia decided to demonstrate the benefits:** National Science Week national office, "Neural Knitworks: Craft a Healthy Brain," https://www.scienceweek.net.au/neural -knitworks-craft-a-healthy-brain/; patterns: https://www.scienceweek.net .au/wp-content/uploads/2014/04/knitworks_patterns.pdf.

129. **Knitters were invited to knit hundreds of neurons:** https://www.facebook .com/neuralknitworks.

131. **Because of this construction, knitting can be used to produce physical models:** Stuart Fox, "Move Over, String Theory, It's Yarn's Turn," *Scienceline* (NYU), May 28, 2008, https://scienceline.org/2008/05 /physics-fox-knitting/.

132. **Such decisions are a crucial part of the design process:** Fox, "Move Over, String Theory."

132. **Knitting is so versatile that it can be used to produce models:** Daina Taimina, "Crocheting Adventures with Hyperbolic Planes," TEDxRiga,

June 14, 2012, video available at https://www.youtube.com/watch?v=D
-AHvZqbMT4.

133. **Professor Taimina's crochet sample:** Taimina, "Crocheting Adventures
with Hyperbolic Planes."

135. **If she succeeds, knitting could help us create new materials for various
uses:** http://meetings.aps.org/Meeting/MAR19/Session/K63.1.

135. **The elasticity comes from how the loops:** Jennifer Ouellette, "Physicists
Are Decoding Math-y Secrets of Knitting to Make Bespoke Materials,"
Ars Technica, March 8, 2019, https://arstechnica.com/science/2019/03
/physicists-are-decoding-math-y-secrets-of-knitting-to-make-bespoke
-materials/.

136. **He makes the case that the art of tracking:** George Dvorsky, "Here Are
Some Essential Survival Skills We've Lost from Our Ancient Ancestors,"
io9, September 23, 2015, https://io9.gizmodo.com/here-are-some
-essential-survival-skills-weve-lost-from-1732594841.

138. **The results showed that among people aged seventy:** Jane E. Brody, "The
Health Benefits of Knitting," *Well* (blog), *New York Times*, January 25,
2016, https://well.blogs.nytimes.com/2016/01/25/the-health-benefits
-of-knitting/.

138. **Black-cab drivers do not use GPS:** Rebecca Maxwell, "Spatial
Orientation and the Brain: The Effects of Map Reading and Navigation,"
GIS Lounge, March 8, 2013, https://www.gislounge.com/spatial
-orientation-and-the-brain-the-effects-of-map-reading-and-navigation/.

Chapter Eight: Let's Knit Together: Restitching Society

147. **At the end of the year, any profit is distributed:** Donna Druchunas,
"Knitting: Hobby or Economic Imperative?" Sheep to Shawl, November
15, 2006, https://sheeptoshawl.com/knitting-softens-impact-worlds
-collide/.

148. **Johnson walked into the studio:** https://www.tengri.co.uk.

153. **According to I Knit's website:** Miss Cellania, "10 Impressive
Yarnbombing Projects," Mental Floss, August 20, 2018, http://
mentalfloss.com/article/77154/10-impressive-yarnbombing-projects.

153. **In Canada, the Rock Vandals:** Nina Elliott, "This Knitted Adventure," *Rock Vandal* (blog), August 7, 2016, https://rockvandals.com/2016/08/07/this-knitted-adventure/.

154. **Their yellow-and-black logo:** Caroline Howard, "Names You Need to Know: Yarn Bombing," *Forbes*, April 30, 2011, https://www.forbes.com/sites/carolinehoward/2011/04/30/names-you-need-to-know-yarn-bombing/#2dad8bdf5c5c.

154. **In Chile, Hombres Tejedores:** "Knitting as a Political Act," *Wooly Ventures* (blog), January 23, 2017, http://www.woolyventures.com/knitting-political-act/.

154. **In Reykjavík, Yarnstormers:** RX Beckett, "The Bus That Yarn Built," Reykjavík Grapevine, September 17, 2012, https://grapevine.is/icelandic-culture/art/2012/09/17/the-bus-that-yarn-built/.

Epilogue: All You Need Is Love

159. **an amazing story of knitting:** https://www.bbc.com/news/av/uk-46595743/knitting-after-grief-leads-to-love.

CREDITS

All patterns shown have been tested and knit by Cristina Longati of Il Caffè dei Gomitoli (www.ilcaffedeigomitoli.it; Facebook: /ilcaffedeigomitoli; Instagram: @ilcaffedeigomitoli), in collaboration with Maglialenta of Grazia (Instagram: @maglialenta).

Pussy Power Hat: Adapted from Kat Coyle for the Pussyhat Project, https://www.pussyhatproject.com/knit.

Wig Hat: Created by Megan Reardon, https://www.ravelry.com/patterns/library/hallowig.

World War I and II Service Socks: Published by the *Star Weekly*, Toronto, 1942; adapted by Grazia Baravelli and Cristina Longati.

Phrygian Cap: Created by Alexandria Bee, https://www.ravelry.com/patterns/library/phrygian-cap.

Unisex Vest: https://www.collectorsweekly.com/articles/yarn-bombs-in-the-70s-knitting-was-totally-far-out/; adapted by Grazia Baravelli and Cristina Longati.

Bikini: Created by Grazia Baravelli and Cristina Longati.

Rastafarian Hat: Created by Grazia Baravelli and Cristina Longati.

Rib Stitch Poppy: Created by Grazia Baravelli and Cristina Longati.

Brain Hat: Adapted from Kathy Doherty, https://www.ravelry.com/patterns/library/thinking-cap; adapted by Grazia Baravelli and Cristina Longati.

Heart: Created by Grazia Baravelli and Cristina Longati.

© Roberto Vettorato

ABOUT THE AUTHOR

Loretta Napoleoni is a lifelong avid knitter who learned to knit as a child in Italy from her grandmother; she is also an economist, consultant, commentator, and bestselling author. Her books on global financing; terrorism; economics and social change since 9/11; and the economies of Europe, China, and North Korea have been translated into twenty-one languages. Through her work with several international organizations, the commodities market, and as a frequent lecturer, she has traveled the world—with knitting projects in tow. She was a Fulbright scholar at Johns Hopkins University's Paul H. Nitze School of Advanced International Studies in Washington, DC, and a Rotary Scholar at the London School of Economics. She holds a master's degree in international relations and economics and a doctorate in economics. She splits her time between London and Rome, with annual visits to the United States.